Comforting the Bereaved Through Listening and Positive Responding

Comforting the Bereaved Through Listening and Positive Responding

What Are the Bereaved Trying to Tell Us?

Dr. Dee Stern, L.C.P.C., PsyD

Copyright © 2022 Dr. Dee Stern, L.C.P.C., PsyD.

All rights reserved. No part of this book may be used or reproduced by any means, graphic, electronic, or mechanical, including photocopying, recording, taping or by any information storage retrieval system without the written permission of the author except in the case of brief quotations embodied in critical articles and reviews.

This book is a work of non-fiction. Unless otherwise noted, the author and the publisher make no explicit guarantees as to the accuracy of the information contained in this book and in some cases, names of people and places have been altered to protect their privacy.

Archway Publishing books may be ordered through booksellers or by contacting:

Archway Publishing
1663 Liberty Drive
Bloomington, IN 47403
www.archwaypublishing.com
844-669-3957

Because of the dynamic nature of the Internet, any web addresses or links contained in this book may have changed since publication and may no longer be valid. The views expressed in this work are solely those of the author and do not necessarily reflect the views of the publisher, and the publisher hereby disclaims any responsibility for them.

Any people depicted in stock imagery provided by Getty Images are models, and such images are being used for illustrative purposes only. Certain stock imagery © Getty Images.

ISBN: 978-1-6657-1624-6 (sc)
ISBN: 978-1-6657-1625-3 (e)

Library of Congress Control Number: 2021924900

Print information available on the last page.

Archway Publishing rev. date: 01/27/2022

I dedicate this book to all the bereaved, especially those who are not listened to, those who are forgotten and pushed aside, and those who are struggling and searching for an end to their emptiness and sadness as they look for a "new normal" in their worlds of chaos.

I dedicate this work to all the nurses, physicians, caregivers, psychologists, families, and friends of the bereaved who have taken the time to sit and listen to them through their pain.

It is my hope that someday those who have *not* yet taken the time to listen to what the bereaved are saying will decide to take the time to listen, understand, and think before they speak to the bereaved, thereby causing them less pain and turmoil than they are already experiencing.

CONTENTS

Acknowledgments ix
Introduction xi

1. The Definition of Grief 1
2. Grief in Adults and Older Adults 10
3. Grief in Children and Adolescents 22
4. Sibling Grief 32
5. Grief and Those Who Have Developmental Disabilities 40
6. The Death of a Pet and Pets Grieve Too 47
7. Grief of Family and Friends of Those Who
   Have Died by Suicide 56
8. Grief and Loss in the Workplace 67
9. The Language of Bereavement 76
10. Triggers—Anniversaries, Birthdays, Holidays 82
11. Disenfranchised Grief and Ambiguous Loss 88
12. Funeral Etiquette and Religious Customs 95

Conclusion 105
Appendix A: Mad Bag 107
Appendix B: "The Dash" 113
Appendix C: Grief and the Holidays 115
Appendix D: Why Don't We Say Their Name 121
Glossary 125
Bibliography 129
Annotated References 139

ACKNOWLEDGMENTS

I would like to thank and express a great deal of gratitude to those friends and colleagues, as well as students, who encouraged me to write this book, especially those who encouraged me to continue when I had given up.

I would especially like to thank those without whose help and encouragement this book would never have been started, much less finished:

Janet Zimmerman, a close friend and my tech support, who put up with my frustrations with the computer and who supported me when things seemed so bleak. Without Janet's assistance and encouragement, I would never have been able to comprehend the workings of the computer and proceed with this project.

Linda Hughes, a good friend and computer wizard who helped me with my illustrations and zip folder and other computer concerns.

Fr. Steven Janoski, a friend and colleague, who constantly encouraged me to begin and finish this material and who always stood by me when I was ready to give up.

Rev. Joe Eby, a friend and colleague, who encouraged me and found GTF for me online and suggested very strongly that I should check it out.

Jeff Koester, a physical therapist, whose friendship, enthusiasm, interest in my project, and his many encouraging words gave me the courage to continue and finish this project.

Arlene Dittberner, a close friend, who helped me by listening and believing in me.

To my former students, who called me to task to finish my doctoral studies as well as this book and to practice what I preach, "Not to give up no matter what."

Dr. Ann V. Graber, my project consultant, without whose support, gentle encouragement, corrections, listening ability, and especially saying yes to being my project coordinator (even with her very busy schedule). Without her, this book would never have been completed.

My grief and suicide support groups, who encouraged me to tell their stories with the hope that someday, someone would listen to them and not use clichés, euphemisms, and metaphors when speaking to them about their deceased loved ones.

INTRODUCTION

As a grief therapist and a licensed clinical professional counselor (LCPC) doing private practice; a chaplain at HSHS St. John's hospital, where I facilitate three grief support groups and the SOS (Survivors of Suicide—for families and friends of those whose loved ones have completed a suicide) group; facilitated a SIDS group, and as a instructor who taught psychology and death and dying courses at Benedictine University and Lincoln College and as a parish/bereavement minister at Little Flower Church, I have heard many painful stories over the years that were related to me by the bereaved. I have heard the pain, anger, and hurt in their stories and voices as they shared their experiences. I also witnessed firsthand what this anger and hurt felt like when my parents, grandparents, brother, and my beagles, Dirky and Max, died, as well as friends and colleagues. I have heard many euphemisms, clichés, and even metaphors as others have. I have also felt the anger and hurt and wondered *why* or *how* people could say the things they say to those who are bereaved.

Because I am a grief therapist and a LCPC, everyone assumed I would be over my grief in a few weeks because "I knew how to grieve" and because I "needed to get over it and move on." First of all, you never get *over* a death, but you can get *through* it. How sad to believe that so many individuals actually felt that way and expressed that to me. It has been many years since these deaths have occurred, but I can still remember the negative things said to me and the people who said them.

I believe that these people and others like them are good, well-meaning individuals who just do not know what to say. They just say the first things that come to their minds and feel that they are bringing comfort to the bereaved. Instead, they are causing anger, pain, and hurt to those who may receive their greetings.

In my grief support and SOS groups, I have seen and heard the bereaveds' pain as they share condolences in phrases like these:

- "Bob was sick—but you knew he was going to die."
- "Aren't you glad you didn't have a chance to bond with or get close to your baby before it died?"
- "He was old and was going to die; he is in a better place now."
- "You are finally free to do whatever you want now that you don't have to go to the hospital or nursing home anymore."
- "You are young enough that you can still have another baby."
- "You are young enough to marry again. Remember, there are others out there just looking for a nice person like you."
- "Remember, you have other children who still need you; you have to be strong for all of them."

Advice to a young child or teen:

- "You must not cry; you are the head of the family now."
- "Be strong for your mother. She really needs you now."
- "Be a good example for your other brothers and sisters, and don't bother your mother. She has a lot to worry about."
- "It was only a pet; you can always get another one."

I believe most people really do not know how to act or what to say to someone who has experienced a death. However, I do not believe that families, friends, and colleagues are the only ones who are at fault; professionals are just as guilty of using this kind of language with their patients. Many of these professionals feel that if the bereaved are just given some medications, they will be fine; unfortunately, many professionals overmedicate the bereaved and cause them to feel nothing, which often extends their mourning and causes even more problems in the long run.

It would be better if the bereaved could just feel they are being heard, know where to go for help, know that what they are feeling is normal grief and that they are not going crazy, not feel that they must be "over their loss" in a few weeks, and not to take what others say personally. Hopefully, others will catch on to the idea of listening to the bereaved and will pass this message on to someone else when they become bereaved themselves.

Remember, offering a hug or saying, "Your loved one will be missed" or "We are thinking of and praying for you," means a great deal to someone who has experienced a death. A cliché, euphemism, or metaphor causes more pain, hurt, and anger that unfortunately may never be forgotten or forgiven.

CHAPTER 1

The Definition of Grief

What is grief? According to *Merriam-Webster*, *grief* is a "deep and poignant distress caused by or as if by bereavement." *Deep* we can understand. *Poignant* relates to feelings—deeply touching or piercing feelings. Bereavement comes from the word *bereave*, which is to deprive of something or to take away. So, basically, grief is the gamut of feelings we have when we are deprived of something or someone, especially something or someone we love. Grief is the term most often used when a death has occurred that describes how those who remain are feeling as a result of this loss. Grief is a journey, an ebb and flow of emotions that changes over time as a person adjusts to the fact that someone or a situation they have been used to has irrevocably changed.

Grief is a normal reaction to any kind of loss and can affect a person's entire being—emotions, physical responses, thoughts, behaviors, spirituality, and even social interactions. Emotionally, people may be sad; they may cry a lot. They might feel angry or guilty ("If only I had not done this" or "If only I could have done that" or "I should have [fill in the blank]" or have other thoughts about redoing the past to have a different outcome). Those who are grieving often feel numb or may literally be in shock, especially immediately after the death of their loved ones.

Physically, the bereaved may be tired or frail or have aches and pains all over their bodies, including chest pains, migraines, high blood pressure, a lack of energy, restlessness, and many other physical symptoms. Cognitively, they may feel they cannot function on a daily basis, cannot focus, can't seem to read or do daily chores, or concentrate on anything. They may talk about their own deaths or even wish for them to occur, so that they can be with their loved ones again.

Spiritually, the bereaved may have lost their faith and trust in God; they may even blame God for the death of their loved ones. Spiritual aspects of their lives that had been constant, such as prayer and church attendance or being with their church communities, might fall to the wayside. Behaviorally, they may feel alone, want to be alone, turn inward, or become very outspoken—behaviors that seems opposite of their personalities. They might be afraid to go anywhere or to leave their homes; or, alternately, they might be anxious to leave their homes to get away from their memories. Socially, they may feel alone and lonely; they may not want to be around people, may not return calls, and may feel that no one cares about them.

All this, and more, is normal grief.

Sadly, in our society and culture, we don't seem to handle grief very well—our own or others'. We live in a death-denying society, where many people feel awkward using the literal terms *death*, *dying*, or *dead*. We rarely say that someone has died, and instead use metaphors such as they "passed," "passed away," "passed over," "went to their heavenly reward," "went to meet their Savior," "kicked the bucket," "bought the farm," or a host of other metaphors, euphemisms, or clichés. Perhaps by not actually saying the words *dying*, *death*, or *dead*, we think we are softening the blow or making an uncomfortable and sad truth less stark. That's not necessarily a terrible thing, but too often, we are also denying the reality of death and the human experience of grief.

A century ago, people were born, lived, and died in the same communities. Everyone in a community knew one another and what each person did. Neighbors watched children grow up, get married, and have their own children; then they grew older and eventually died and were buried. When someone in the community died, everyone knew about it. The entire community was affected in some way. Today, in our busy world, we don't seem to have the same connection that we had with our neighbors many years ago. When someone in the neighborhood dies, we may not know them or perhaps even make an effort to contact the family as we might have done in the past. This lack of social support from distant family, acquaintances, coworkers, and neighbors could make it harder for the bereaved to readjust because support must include consolation and empathy, neither of which we see very often today.

Society is also becoming deritualized. Years ago, people wore black arm bands and black dresses (full black for a year, then gray for another year) and put black wreaths on their front doors when a death occurred. You knew simply by looking at a person or a home that they had experienced a death recently. Today, there are fewer traditional visitations, wakes, and funerals and more celebrations of life, graveside services, and cremations without any other kind of service.

It's almost as if the deceased have simply … disappeared. All those activities, though they may honor and respect the person who died, are not really *for* the person who died. They are for those left behind, those who now must figure out how to live life without the deceased.

Today, people seem to spend more time texting, emailing, and calling each other than talking with bereaved friends face-to-face to express their sympathies. Why does this happen? Could it be because people don't know what to say and might think they could cause the bereaved to feel worse? Or is it because the bereaved may talk about their loved ones and begin to cry, and then people won't know what to say or do? Perhaps if people would take the time to visit the bereaved and just sit and listen to them or give them a hug (if they want one), they might realize how much these actions would mean to those who are struggling with the loss of a loved one. Sending a card or going to the visitation, funeral, or celebration of life are other ways to let the bereaved know someone cares about them at this very difficult time in their lives. Another idea would be to take food over to the home of the bereaved. If the food is in a personal container rather than a disposable container, when the dish is empty, this would allow the person to spend a little time talking to the bereaved when a person comes to retrieve their dish.

Perhaps the reason we don't say the words *dying, death,* or *dead* is to avoid the emotional response of grieving. Is this a reaction stemming from our own discomforts or lack of knowing what to say to someone who has experienced the death of someone close? Is it because we don't want to see people cry or be sad, and so we feel we must cheer them up so they can be happy like us? Some people will change the subject rather than talk about death or simply use the avoidance method—not talking to a grieving person until they have moved on or "gotten over their grief."

For a significant period of time, many people who are grieving need and want to maintain some sort of connection with the person who has died. This connection represents an ongoing internal bond with the deceased, allowing that death has changed the relationship but giving the griever an internal representation of the person. This connection often provides comfort, support, and solace for the bereaved. Some examples of connecting with the bereaved loved one might be continuing to wear their wedding band, making a quilt or pillow out of their loved one's clothes, or making a scrapbook or photo album of their loved one's life. After all, even though death ends a life, the relationship is still intact. Mourning releases the bereaved person to continue living a meaningful life without the deceased and without leaving their loved one behind, yet still having that connection that is so often sought after.

A very common question about grief is, *How long?* How long will the bereaved continue to grieve? Many of the bereaved wonder when (or even if) they will stop grieving. The simple answer is: Everyone is different, and everyone grieves differently. Grief takes as long as it takes; there is no real time limit. For some, it is a few months; for others, years; and still for others, it takes a lifetime.

Grief is not something you get "over"; it's something that changes you forever. Think of it as the surgical removal of some part of your body: immediately after surgery, you may be in pain, and it may take time to get back to the daily tasks of living. After surgery, you may spend months doing physical rehabilitation to reach your goals, goals that are "new" because you've had to reattain them. And even though you may eventually be back to 100 percent physically—doing things you love to do and living life to the fullest—you will still have a scar. There is still a part of you that is missing. You are changed. This is the way of grief. You won't have that initial pain forever, but you will always bear the scars of losing someone you love.

Many people may feel that their "primary" grieving is over when they are able to remember their loved ones without the same intensity of pain that they experienced in the past and are able once again to do their daily tasks and invest in their own lives with plans for the future. The first year of bereavement is an especially difficult and challenging time for the bereaved, but often, the second year can be worse because the finality of the first year's experiences comes forward with the stark realization that this is now the way life is. That first year is a year of firsts, such as birthdays, anniversaries, holidays, and "regular" days without their loved ones, typically with lots of support and understanding from family and friends.

However, by the second year, most of that support is gone, and the bereaved are truly on their own. Without the recognition and support of family and friends, and even perhaps having new people in their lives who may not have known their loved ones or know about the loved one's death, that second year can also be harder than the first—especially in terms of loneliness and isolation. As time goes by, the ebb and flow of grief tends to smooth out the places that used to be rough. Remembering the person who died may bring more happy thoughts than sad feelings. However, some of the bereaved may feel that their mourning is never over, and they continue to grieve and mourn. This might be more prevalent when a child has died or when the death was sudden or violent.

Many of the bereaved experience normal grief; however, for some, grief is complicated. Here are four examples of complicated grief:

Chronic grief includes reactions that seem to go on and on and do not come to an appropriate ending. This occurs when the bereaved realize they are not moving along as well as they thought they would. *Delayed grief* reactions refer to suppressed grief that has been stuffed down so deeply inside that they do not (or cannot) deal with their grief until it surfaces again or is set off by some kind of a trigger. *Exaggerated grief* reactions refer to grief that can be excessive or even disabling to the bereaved and could lead to developing phobias, irrational fears, or even physical or psychiatric symptoms. *Masked grief* reactions occur when the bereaved displays a complete lack of grief but experiences problems that seem unrelated to any kind of loss—when, in fact, they are really related.

Complicated grief is more common in certain circumstances. These include a sudden, unanticipated death, especially when it is traumatic, random, or violent; death after a lengthy illness; the death of a child; the perception by the bereaved that the death was preventable; an angry, dependent, or ambivalent relationship between the bereaved and the deceased; prior or concurrent mental health problems, losses, or stresses for the bereaved that were not accommodated; or the bereaved feeling a perceived lack of social support. These situations could easily complicate the bereaved person's ability to adapt to their life without the person who died.

Complicated grief is complicated because it serves to deny, repress, or avoid aspects of the loss, the pain it causes, and the full realization of its implications for the bereaved. It also enables the bereaved to avoid relinquishing their loved ones. Complicated grief is exacerbated by a variety of changes in society's constructs, such as urbanization, secularization, deritualization, violence, availability of guns, social alienation, substance abuse, as well as a sense of hopelessness.

Personality traits or mental health matters, such as insecurity, anxiety, or attachment issues, can also be risks for developing complicated grief. Addressing questions such as: Who died? How close was the deceased to the bereaved? How did the death occur? Was the death sudden or anticipated? What was the quality of the survivor's relationship with the deceased? Was there any unfinished business between the deceased and the bereaved? Were there any prior losses that the bereaved had experienced before this death? Did the death have complications attached to it? These and other questions may be beneficial to help the bereaved avoid complicated grief. The most important factor to consider is, who will ask the questions and listen to the bereaved's responses? Whether that person is a friend, a support group, clergy, or a professional, allowing the bereaved to talk out the answers can go a long way toward helping them through the grieving process in a beneficial way.

Henri Nouwen writes about dealing with loss in his book *Wait for the Lord* and raises these questions: "What do we do with our losses? Are we hiding them? Are we going to live as if they weren't real? Are we going to keep them away from our fellow travelers? Are we going to convince ourselves or others that our losses are little compared to our gains? Are we going to blame someone?" He goes on to say,

> We do all these things most of the time, but there is another possibility: the possibility of mourning. We cannot talk or act them away, but we can shed tears over our losses and allow ourselves to grieve deeply. To grieve is to allow our losses to tear apart feelings of security and safety and lead us to the painful truth of brokenness. Our grief makes us experience the abyss of our own life in which nothing is settled, clear or obvious, but everything is constantly shifting and changing. ...
>
> As we feel the pain of our losses, our grieving hearts open our inner eye to a world in which losses are suffered far beyond our own world of family, friends, and colleagues. It is a world of prisoners, refugees, AIDS patients, starving children, and the countless human beings living in constant fear. Then the pain of our crying hearts connects us with the

moaning and groaning of a suffering humanity. Then our mourning becomes larger than ourselves.

Nouwen is correct when he talks about the connection between individual losses and the suffering of humanity. For when we mourn, we are not alone; rather, we mourn with all those who have ever mourned and will continue to mourn every day of their lives.

Why is it so important to give ourselves permission to grieve and to feel what we feel? Why is it so important to allow others to grieve their losses without telling them to "get over it" or "move on"? Because we all should be able to feel the compassion from others and for others without someone telling us they liked us better when we were happy. When we help someone else, it also helps us to feel better and to find meaning in our lives again. As we grieve, it is important *not* to apologize for what we feel but rather to go through the pain of losing our loved ones so that we can eventually be healed.

Grief is the great equalizer, and no matter who or what we are, or how rich or poor, grief can bring us to our knees. Therefore, feel what you feel and do not let others (especially those who have not experienced a loss) tell you how you *should* feel or when your grief *should* be done. Never apologize for what you feel because you have a right to feel that way. Allow yourself to feel the connection between you and your loved ones and never let them go. Rather, continue to remember them in the weeks and months ahead. For they will always be a part of you, and you will always be part of them.

Chapter References

*Anderson, Robert. *I Never Sang for My Father*. New York: Dramatists Play Service, 1968.

Cable, D. "Grief in the American Culture." In *Living with Grief: Who We Are How We Grieve*, eds. K. J. Doka and J. D. Davidson, 61–70. Philadelphia: Hospice Foundation of America, 2000.

*Clayton, P. J. "Mortality and Morbidity in the First Year of Widowhood." *Archives of General Psychiatry* 30 (1974): 747–750.

Corr, C. A., C. M. Nabe, and D. M. Corr. *Death and Dying, Life and Living*. 3rd ed. Belmont, CA: Wadsworth, 2000.

DeSpelder, L. A., and A. L. Strickland. *The Last Dance: Encountering Death and Dying*. Mountain View, CA: Mayfield, 2014.

Gamino, L., & Ritter, H. (2009). *Ethical practice in grief counseling*. New York: Spring.

*Klass, D., Silverman, P.R., & Nickman, S. L. (1996). *Continuing bonds: New understandings of grief*. Washington, D.C.: Taylor & Francis.

Nouwen, H. (2014). *Wait for the Lord*. Fenton, MO: Creative Communications for the Parish.

*Rando, T. (1993). *The treatment of complicated mourning*. Champaign, IL: Research Press.

*Worden, J. W. (2002). *Grief counseling and grief therapy: A handbook for the mental health practitioner* (3rd ed.). New York: Springer.

* See Annotated References for a short description of this resource.

CHAPTER 2

Grief in Adults and Older Adults

At some point in their lives, most people experience the death of someone they know, whether it is a child, sibling, spouse, parent, grandparent, or friend. As adults, we develop an awareness of mortality, meaning there is an acknowledgment and even an acceptance that no one lives forever. There are several factors that contribute to the development of this middle adulthood awareness of mortality. As we age, we simply can't do the things we did as easily in our teens and early twenties. Our eyesight and hearing might decline; our bones and muscles ache more often; we get tired more easily; and our desires for things that drove us ten, fifteen, or twenty years ago—beauty, power, sex, money—have likely started to diminish.

Once we hit our forties, the mortality rate increases, as does our awareness of and experience with death. This is often because more serious illnesses occur; death—not related to accidents or suicide—occurs more often to peers, coworkers, friends, and family. To the middle-aged person, the prospect of death becomes the haunting thought that they may be robbed of the opportunity to achieve their goals and truly enjoy the fruits of their achievements, perhaps causing a midlife crisis that, in turn, could cause the person to search for meaning in life that perhaps was not there before.

When adults in midlife experiences a loss, they have a lot to deal with. The death happens, and they recognize this fact, but they often also have to "be the adult" and take care of immediate concerns (e.g., informing others, making arrangements, as well as settling the estate). Their "reactive" grief, how they respond to the death of this particular individual, will likely cover a gamut of emotions and reactions, such as shock, denial, anger, and depression. These feelings and emotions may come at different times, with different intensities, and may be repeated. In other words, just because someone has expressed anger about a death doesn't mean that person can't or won't experience more anger in the future.

Existential grief, on the other hand, is a more abstract feeling or a knowing—often precipitated by the loss one has just experienced—that at some point, the surviving individual him- or herself will die. This may cause deep introspection or even depression, ending with the focus on more of the survivors' own lives, successes (or lack thereof), goals, and dreams, rather than on the loss of the person who has died.

Another common midlife experience is when adults begin to experience their own parents' aging and dying, as well as their parents' friends dying. No matter how old you are, when a parent dies, you feel there is less of a buffer against death. When both parents die, it feels as though you're an "orphan" as an adult; you automatically become the "older generation," and it's harder to deny your own mortality.

This awareness can cause a paradoxical situation in which older adults (aged sixty-five and older) feel the necessity to talk to their middle-aged children about their needs and wants concerning their deaths, but their children may feel threatened or even frightened about the idea of their parents' deaths and therefore want to avoid talking about them. The children's fears may include having no one to walk them down the aisle at a wedding, no one to talk to for advice, and no one to share the grandkids' significant milestones with—such as their first steps, the first time they say *grandma* or *grandpa*, or when they graduate from grade school, high school, and beyond.

Our parents represent our pasts, and when they die, it is like our pasts are gone. Who will be there to tell us about what it was like for us, growing up? When there is a question about the past, who do we go to for answers? Some families are very close and adult children depend on their parents to be their supports; the thought of not having them around often causes the adult child to avoid discussing the death of their parents. Often, when parents approach the subject of death, the adult child simply laughs it off and changes the subject because of the many fears they may have. If elderly parents would like to continue this conversation with their adult children, they may need to wait for a time when their children are ready to listen. Parents can begin plans on their own, without their adult children's input. This could cause some concerns in the future, however; sometimes, these plans cannot wait for their adult children to be ready to talk. These plans often include making or updating a will, cleaning out or downsizing their homes, or designating a power of attorney for medical needs.

When a Spouse Dies

Losing a spouse is difficult because spouses typically become dependent on each other for conversation, love, and shared tasks around their home over the years of their marriage. Loneliness is one of the most difficult emotions, among many other things that a surviving spouse faces on a regular basis. It just doesn't go away.

Add to that the "division of labor" that typically occurs in a household: One spouse may have done the laundry, cooking, and cleaning, while the other took care of the yard, paid the bills, and made sure there was gas in the car. Once a spouse dies, the survivor must learn to cope the best way they know how, which is devastating for some because the survivor may have no idea what to do or where to go and could end up not paying bills, running out of gas, or, more drastically, abusing drugs, alcohol, gambling, and going on buying sprees for things they really don't need.

Communicating with extended family members may fall to the wayside simply because the surviving spouse isn't aware of anniversaries, birthdays, or the need to relay details about the family to others. Connecting with extended family and friends becomes a chore or an overwhelming responsibility that the surviving spouse isn't used to handling, and they might opt to simply let things go.

Maintaining a connection with the spouse who has died is another difficult topic. Many survivors choose to wear a special piece of jewelry or continue to wear their wedding bands. There also may be a favorite shirt or another article of clothing that is a comforting reminder of the deceased spouse. One option for using these items is to have a pillow, blanket, or another item made from these memory-holders. Another idea is for children or grandchildren to help the bereaved spouse put together a picture album or a scrapbook of the deceased. Go out for dinner at the deceased loved one's favorite restaurant on their birthday or anniversary. All these things can help with loneliness and keep a connection with the deceased loved one.

As for activities to get the surviving spouse out of the house and socializing with others, a grief support group, where they can meet others who will listen to and understand their story, might be beneficial. Volunteering, doing things for others at a hospital, library, school, or church, is another way to help a surviving spouse regain some social interaction.

Part of the difficulty with losing a spouse is that, often, the couple have been "we" for so long that it is hard to determine what just a "me" looks like. After a death, a person's sense of self changes and begins to take on a new meaning. The surviving spouse has to figure out who they are now, alone—even to the point of wondering if the person still qualifies as a husband or wife, since the spouse has died. "Who am I?" becomes a huge question, as the person must speak up for themselves and make decisions about what to do now that they are on their own.

This new "freedom" may seem exciting in certain circumstances, but to a surviving spouse, it may be overwhelming and frightening. Although it's important that a spouse and a family share memories of their loved ones, having a community take part in remembrance is also very healing. Holding an annual event to raise money for a worthy cause, such as a golf outing or one of the deceased's favorite causes, celebrating significant birthdays or anniversaries, memorializing them with plaques or trees or other permanent items, and participating in activities to honor their memories, are all examples of ways community memorials benefit all involved.

Men and Women Grieve Differently

Men and women grieve differently—even when facing the same loss—simply because their emotions are uniquely wired. This is why women may assume that a man is not grieving or doesn't care, when, in fact, he is struggling with his pain in his own way. He simply may not be sure of what to do with his pain because he believes he has to be strong for his family and himself.

Traditionally, societal norms says that women can feel what they feel—"cry, scream, yell"—but men must keep a "stiff upper lip." Society also says that it's a man's job to protect his family; a women's job is to nurture her family. Some men feel they are a failure for not being able to protect their families when a death occurs. Women usually feel very comfortable expressing their feelings and telling their stories to others, whereas many men may be uncomfortable with expressing their feelings. Thus, they end up keeping everything to themselves, which may cause problems down the road as they must deal with hidden or stuffed emotions, or they may occasionally confide in other men.

It is important to be more understanding of both male and female reactions and not judge what someone may be feeling. Grief is a time for listening and compassion, not for giving advice—especially if you haven't been asked for it—and for being patient and present to the bereaved, because you certainly don't know what they may have experienced or are experiencing at a specific point in time.

A huge part of losing a spouse is the loss of companionship. This longing for companionship, as well as the loneliness the survivors are feeling, is why some people will date or remarry soon after losing a spouse. This may create difficulties in relationships with children or the deceased spouse's family. It may even cause the surviving spouse to feel guilty. Many bereaved people just want company—someone to talk to or go out to dinner with, to go to a show or on a trip with, but not necessarily someone to marry again. When—if—they are ready, perhaps giving them freedom and support is what, in the long run, is better for the bereaved. Don't push, but don't hold them back, either. Let them take the steps, if they want to, to move forward with their lives.

Older Adults and Grief

In later life (ages sixty-five and older), the awareness of finitude—knowing there is a finish—can cause a review of one's life, as well as a desire to plan, as much as is possible, for a good and appropriate death. This "life review" can be a positive activity, but it can also create some depressive attitudes. The older adult might focus on loneliness, especially if a spouse, siblings, friends, or others of their generation have already died. If they struggle with managing everyday tasks, the frustrations can compound.

In general, the bereaved realize that the sense of order in their worlds are being challenged over and over. For the older generation, their own physical health and abilities to get around in their communities may help to determine their new coping skills and how they go about doing them. It is important for family and friends to ask how they can help, and for the bereaved to accept their invitations.

Many in the older generation today are not only burying their children but also raising their grandchildren. This change in the lives of the older generation can be considered a time of transition because it has become a change in status and a shift in roles. The bereaved must now learn to live in a changed world where they are not only grieving but are also learning how to help their grandchildren grieve. They may now be taking their grandchildren to school and picking them up as well as taking them to practices for music, sports, scouts, and to their friends' houses. Their lives have changed. Their realities of what life looks like at their age may be vastly different than what they had envisioned years before.

The world of the bereaved is constantly changing and so must their ways of coping. When the numbing feelings of shock and disbelief begin to disappear, reality sets in. This is often the time when many people feel depressed and are not sure what to do to or where to get help.

Adult children may become overprotective. Although the bereaved may try to avoid the feelings they have, they must look for new ways to cope; this will take help from those around them. Going to a grief support group will help the bereaved learn more about their grief and how to deal with it, as well as provide the opportunity to meet others who are struggling as they are. The group will help them to understand that grief takes as long as it takes and that there is no set time limit, as many others may think. They will discover it is okay to feel what they feel and that they should not to feel overwhelmed because others may be pushing them to move on.

They will come to realize that most people do not know what to say to them, and therefore they often say the wrong thing, such as telling them to get over it or to move on—or even, "I liked you better before, when you were happy." These words can be hurtful and sting for a long time, as well as cause the bereaved more pain, confusion, or anxiety.

Over time, the older generation will learn to deal with the pain of their grief. They become in charge of their grief rather than having their grief be in charge of them. They may still feel the pain of loss, but they now feel a different connection to their loved ones and to many of their friends and family who have already died.

There are many ways the older generation can be helped in their grief journeys, but it is up to them to make the final decisions as to how they will allow themselves to grieve and to continue living their new lives. They should not be forced to attend a group or go to a counselor or doctor if they do not feel this would help them. Forcing someone to attend a grief support group or see a counselor often backfires; they may attend once, but once they've "tried it," they feel they've satisfied the agreement with whomever forced them, and they won't come back—even if it ultimately would have helped them.

The benefits of support groups include the chance to meet others going through similar experiences, the opportunities to have others listen to and legitimize their stories and feelings, learning information that could help them in their mourning, and perhaps even finding or becoming a role model in the group and, in turn, having the opportunity to help others. Attendance in these groups gives those who are grieving the opportunity to "repeople their lives." Developing these types of resources helps them realize that the goal isn't to "recover" from or "get over" their grief, but rather to realize that they will be changed by it and that they will, in fact, get through it.

Suicide in Grieving Older Adults

However, for those who are not moving through the process of grieving well, suicide, especially in older adults, is an outcome that happens more often than it should. Statistically, white males over the age of eighty-five have the highest suicide rate of any age group, and it is the thirteenth leading cause of death for those over the age of sixty-five. The question is, why? A simple review of the topics in this chapter provides the answer. Older adults struggle with a variety of negative emotions, including despair, loneliness, fear, anxiety, and depression when they have lost their spouses, friends, and cohorts. They may fear the potential of future illnesses and what those might entail. They may have reviewed their own lives and feel they didn't "do" anything of importance. They don't want to be a burden, but they feel that many end-of-life decisions may be out of their control.

Additionally, substance abuse disorders can create a climate for suicide. Alcohol abuse as well as depression in older people may be overlooked by professional caregivers and families. Overmedication for actual medical problems—diabetes, dementia, heart disease, and depression—can also contribute to an older adult's lack of energy, interest, and emotional investment in living. Simply not taking a needed medication is another willful act of control an older adult may choose that has life-threatening potential.

Factors not related to substance abuse that could put older people at risk for suicide include feelings of hopelessness, social circumstances (either present or future), illnesses, and loss of physical functionality (e.g., difficulty walking, sleeplessness, or the inability to care for themselves). While older adults can deal with the loss of a loved one in a healthy manner, ungrieved losses and feelings of hopelessness could possibly trigger suicidal thoughts, which is why it is so important for the bereaved to get the help they need when these and other feelings arise.

Any adult is at risk for suicide when a loved one dies. It is up to those who are around them daily to look for signs of deep or abnormal grief and help them get the help they need before it is too late. When a loved one commits suicide and the family is struggling to deal with this additional loss, it is important to find a suicide support group for the family to help them through this very difficult and painful time in their lives. The grief from a suicide is more intense and complicated than regular grief. The question of *why?* is always at the forefront, compounded by the emotions of guilt, anger, and disbelief.

Helping Adults and Older Adults Grieve

The bereaved often struggle with the fact that many family members and friends do not mention their loved ones who have died. It is almost as if their loved ones never existed. Family and friends must realize it is not only okay but also helpful to talk about the bereaveds' loved ones. Hearing their loved ones' names and sharing stories about them are extremely beneficial. When their names are forbidden or stories about them are avoided in a futile effort to bypass "a sad subject," it seems to the bereaved that no one cares about them or their loved ones.

The bereaved are fragile people who need to know that their loved ones will not be forgotten and that someone cares about them and their loved ones who died. Take time to listen to their pain; don't change the subject or ignore them—or, even worse, walk right out of their lives until they are over it.

What can we do to help adults and older adults with their grief? The most important thing we can do for the bereaved (really, at any age) is to *listen to them*. Allow them to tell their stories over and over. Let them know you care about them and their deceased loved ones. When you have the opportunity, mention their loved ones' names and share your own stories. Don't tell them to "get over it" or to "move on." If you want to know how they are doing, ask them how their days are going, not about how they are. If you ask a recently bereaved person how they are, their comment might range from "How do you think I am? My loved one died!" to "I'm fine," when actually, they are having a difficult time and don't feel they can share that with you. Often, when the bereaved say they are fine, it's difficult to know for sure how they really are. They do not want to be a burden and therefore are careful about what they say and who they say it to.

However, if you ask them how their days or weeks are going, they seem to understand that you are really concerned about them and not trying to rush them through their grief, and they will feel free to answer you honestly. Please be patient with the bereaved, and don't expect them to function in a normal way for several months. Remember, grief takes as long as it takes and cannot be rushed. Allow them to cry if they need to, but don't give them insincere platitudes or tell them they are okay and that they will be fine, because you don't know that.

Practical things to help the bereaved include stopping by to check on them, taking a meal over (Note: Instead of using disposable containers to make things easier, use your own containers; this automatically provides another opportunity to spend a few minutes with them when you return to pick them up.), cutting their grass, helping with household chores, or going to the grocery store with or for them. Even just sending a card or calling them now and then helps more than you can imagine. Listening and being present with them and just letting them tell their stories or cry—without giving them any advice—is really the most important thing you can do.

Chapter References

Anderson, R. (1974). Notes of a survivor. In S. B. Green (Ed.), *The patient, death and the family*. New York: Oxford University Press.

Blow, F. C. (1998). *Substance abuse among older adults: Treatment improvement protocol*. [Brochure series #26]. Rockville, MD: U.S. Dept. of Health and Human Services.

Brogden, M. (2001). *Genocide*. London and Philadelphia: Jessica Kingsley Publishers.

Campbell, S., & Silverman, P. R. (1996). *Widower: When men are left alone*. Amityville, New York: Baywood.

Conwell, Y. (2001). Suicide in later life: A review and recommendations for prevention. *Suicide and Life-threatening behavior*, Suppl: 31: 32–47.

Kastenbaum, R., & Aisenberg, R. (1976). The psychology of death. New York: Springer.

Lund, D. A. (1989). Older bereaved spouses: Research with practical applications. New York: Taylor & Francis.

Marshall, V. (1980). Last Chapter: A sociology of aging and dying. Monterey, CA: Brooks/Cole.

Moss, M., & Moss. S. (1983). The impact of parental death on middle aged children. *Omega: Journal of Death & Dying, 14,* 65–67.

Motto, J. (1999). Critical points in the assessment and management of suicide risk. In D. G. Jacobs (Ed.), *The Harvard Medical School* guide to suicide assessment and intervention (pp. 224–238). San Francisco: Jossey-Bass

Osgood, N. (1992). *Suicide in later life.* New York: Lexington Books.

Pearson, J. (2000). Suicidal behavior in later life. In R. Maris, S. J. Canetto, J. McIntosh, J. Silverman (Eds.), *Review of Suicidology 2000* (pp. 202–225). New York: Guilford.

Piaget, J. (1954). *The construction of reality in the child.* New York: Basic Books.

Shneidman, E. S. (1993). Suicide as psychache. *Journal of Nervous and Mental Diseases,* 181(3), 147–149.

Silverman, P. R., & Klass, D. (1996). Introduction: What's the problem? *Continuing bonds: New understandings in grief.* Washington, D.C.: Taylor & Francis.

Stephenson, J. (1985). *Death, grief and mourning: Individual and social realities.* New York: Free Press.

Tamir, L. (1982). *Men in their forties: The transition to middle age.* New York: Springer.

CHAPTER 3

Grief in Children and Adolescents

How can we help children and teens when they are grieving the death of a loved one or close friend? How do children act when they are grieving, and what can families, counselors, or friends do to help them get through those tough times? What should a child be told about death? Is it okay to soften the reality of death by not saying the words *died*, *death*, or *dead*? Is it okay not to talk about death and instead act as if everything is okay? Should children even go to the visitations or funerals of their loved ones?

These and other similar questions can cause families great distress because they want to protect their children and teens and keep the bad things in life away from them as much as possible. Unfortunately, in these particular circumstances, this strategy ends up being a paradox: Adults and parents really want to protect their children and teens from the harsh realities and difficult emotions surrounding death, yet they often end up causing more pain and trouble, both now and in the future, by not allowing their children to feel what they feel and talk honestly about death.

Honesty is the best policy in all circumstances, especially in those related to death and dying. Children need to be told the truth about when a loved one is dying, and they need to be allowed to express their feelings. They need to hear the truth in terms they understand. They should be allowed to ask questions. They should be allowed to visit or talk to the dying person (if they want to), whether their loved ones are at home or at a hospital, nursing home, or hospice facility. They should be allowed to say goodbye to their loved ones or friends.

Children understand a lot more than adults give them credit for. They are called "forgotten survivors" because many adults think children are too young to understand. Adults don't want to upset their children, and in reality, it may be that it's too difficult for the adult to talk about the death. The old saying that "children should be seen and not heard" is a false statement because children not only need to be seen, but heard as well. Being allowed to express what is truly in their hearts and minds is very important for their emotional health.

However, if the child is not ready to talk right away, please don't push them to talk. Children need to process and think, just as adults do. Instead, be there when they are ready to talk and let them know they can come to you at any time.

Behaviors to Watch For

Often, children will act out at home, school, or even with their friends when they are troubled because they don't know what to do with all their feelings. Acting out can consist of many different emotions and behaviors, such as becoming aggressive—or even regressive, such as reverting back to bedwetting or thumb-sucking. They may become very angry and sad, turn inward, or strike out at other children, teachers, or their parents. Children may feel guilty because of their thoughts or what they said to their loved ones before the person died. As a result, they may have deep guilt and feel it was their fault when their loved ones died, which is why it is so important for adults to listen to children. They may cry a lot or not at all; they may not want to eat, or, conversely, they may eat more; they may be afraid to sleep; or they may be afraid to mention the name of the person who died, for fear it will upset everyone around them.

All these behaviors and emotions are possible, but it doesn't mean that any—or all—of them will occur. The expression of feelings through these behaviors likely depends on how the child is told of the death from the beginning and how the child (and the subject of death) is treated later. Has the child been allowed or encouraged to talk about the death? Have they been told not to say the deceased's name? The positive or negative instructions or impressions children receive after the death of a loved one will affect them far longer than many adults realize. They need to be told the truth and to be heard, not dismissed because they are children.

Emotions can overwhelm children to the point that expressing themselves physically is the only release they can find. If children are very aggressive and strike out at others, parents can provide pillows, punching bags, or mad bags (see the appendix for instructions to make one) for them to hit to express their aggression and anger. As long as it is safe and they can't harm themselves or others, providing a physical way of releasing emotions can be very helpful.

Often, children are unable to tell someone what they are thinking or feeling, but they can draw a picture. This is the basic premise of art therapy, and it has been shown to be very enlightening as well as helpful. Take note of the colors a child uses when coloring or drawing a picture; this will provide insight into what is going on inside of them. For example, red means anger or passion, orange can express rage, and black is usually death. Blue and yellow are usually upbeat colors. Sometimes they will just scribble back and forth with a black crayon and use a lot of red and orange as well. They do not have to say a word or draw something recognizable, because they have said it all in their color choices. An older child might be able to talk and draw at the same time and not even realize the things they are telling you. Play therapy is another good way to get children to express their feelings. Using a sand tray or doing puppet shows helps them to understand what has happened and how they can learn to cope with the loss of their loved ones. School-age children have a lot to deal with after the death of a loved one. Their own emotions, the changes that have taken place at home—either temporarily or permanently—fears of the unknown or what life will be like, plus the normal stresses of interacting with classmates, learning new information, and performing necessary and expected tasks all mix together in a child's mind. Any one of these or other factors can trigger an unexpected or atypical reaction from the child.

At a grieving child's school, teachers and counselors should be made aware that there has been a death so they are prepared for potential changes in the child's behavior. Teachers should not expect top performance from these children for several weeks or months. These bereaved children may lose friends, make new ones, cry a lot in class, or become disruptive by shouting out loud, striking out at other students, or just plain be annoying. These are normal reactions and should not be ignored, but rather dealt with at the time by talking to the child and listening to them express the pain of emptiness and loneliness caused by the recent death. What these children learn and the way they are treated in this situation—good or bad—will stay with them for the rest of their lives and could become a foundation for future losses in their lives.

Children ask a lot of questions, regardless of their ages. Responses should be truthful and accurate, even if stated in simple terms. Because their realms of understanding are not often mature, using metaphors, euphemisms, or clichés can be not only confusing, but frightening for children. For example, when someone says that "Grandpa is in a better place," "Grandma is in heaven," "Dad died in his sleep," or even "Mommy was really sick and she died," they can take the message very literally and want to go visit Grandma or Grandpa in that "better place" or "heaven," be afraid to go to sleep, or even more afraid of getting sick because they could die, too.

Children can also be very literal because they do not yet have the resources or life experiences to grasp how the bigger world operates outside of their understanding. They often don't know how to integrate loss into their worlds. They will fill in these gaps of understanding with thoughts like, "I should never have told Bobby I hated him and wished he would die, because now he is dead and it is all my fault." This is where adults need to explain honestly and simply that no matter what the child thought or felt before the person died, the death wasn't their fault. If left unaddressed, this thinking can continue and become internalized for the child, especially if the adults in their lives are so caught up in their own grief that they are unable to help their children understand the truth about the situation.

Many adults do not realize that their children and grandchildren remember their deceased loved ones during birthdays and holidays, and they may want to talk about them or look at pictures of them. Because so many adults want to avoid upsetting their children or grandchildren—or because they still are grieving themselves—they don't talk about their loved ones during these times because they want everyone to be happy. However, children may feel frustrated because no one mentions their deceased parents or grandparents or tells stories about them. Instead of avoiding the subject altogether, this could be a good time for everyone to remember and tell stories of their deceased loved ones.

Teens and Grief

An adolescent is someone who is not a child anymore, but who is not yet an adult. Is it any wonder teens struggle so much with who they are and what they are supposed to do in life? Caught between being a child and adulthood, adolescence is a time of life when death, loss, and grief can make a profound impact on a person. Teens can get caught in the middle when a death occurs because they understand more than children, yet they still feel the pain and experience the feelings of abandonment just like others do. They can grasp more of the specific details about a loved one's death—such as how an illness progresses, how age affects the body, or how severe injuries can't be overcome, for example—so they are more equipped to reason out why death happens and what it means. But the emotional maturity and reactions, and the expectations put upon teens cannot be the same as those of an adult. Their maturity isn't at the same level. Adolescents could give the impression that they are able to deal with their grief, but in reality, they are just as confused and anxious about it as children and adults.

Generally speaking, teens don't think of death the same way that others do. They may participate in risky behaviors because they feel invincible. The broad range of teens' attitudes toward death is seen in the entertainment media in video games, movies, and even some music. In essence, many adolescents tend to live in the moment and do not always understand personal threats associated with death—either that it could happen to someone they know or to themselves, or that it will affect their lives.

Teens may try to figure out what is going on in their families and try to fix or take control of the situation. They often think that by becoming the woman or man of the family, they can protect and help the remaining parent—sometimes to the point of being overly protective or helpful. Unfortunately, without thinking, adults will sometimes say to teens, "You have to be strong for your mother/father/sibling." Adults often do not realize the burden or pressure they are putting on their teens by the things they say to them when a death occurs.

Teens need to know that their grief is respected and that it will be understood by those who listen to them. They experience changes in their lives perhaps even more so than others do, because as teens, they are dealing with so many other issues in their lives. It may be very difficult for them to take on the responsibility of a death all alone, and they need to be heard. They may experience physical reactions such as stomachaches, headaches, decreases or increases in appetite, or changes in sleeping habits due to worry. And when they do sleep, they may have dreams that upset them. They may be lethargic, even avoiding activities they normally enjoy.

Emotionally, they may become even more sensitive than usual or very quiet and withdrawn from everyone and everything. They may experience survivor's guilt (especially if the deceased is a friend or a sibling), fear, regret, loneliness, anger, and apathy. They may attempt to commit suicide because of the guilt they feel or the bewilderment about what has happened in their lives. They may feel out of control and be too embarrassed to express their feelings to anyone or fear that they may cry in front of their peers and be rejected.

Psychological changes may have them acting contrary to their "normal" states of being. If they were good students before, now they may not do assignments and their grades may drop; they may daydream even more than usual, be very forgetful, or unable to focus or pay attention in class. Activities that they love, such as sports or music or art, may fall to the wayside or become obsessions.

Socially, teens may withdraw from their friends and families, and they may not be interested in doing any activities. They may turn to drugs or alcohol or criminal activities. Spiritually, they may blame God or become angry with him or withdraw from church and other religious activities. They will probably ask such questions as: "Why did this happen?" or "Why did it happen to her or him?" It is very important to listen to these adolescents as they express their feelings and let them know that someone cares about them and will be there for them. Allow them to talk and express what is in their hearts and minds without judgment or a sense of how they should or shouldn't feel.

What may help: These bereaved adolescents may cope by keeping a journal of their thoughts, listening to music, writing a song in memory of their loved ones, writing poetry or prose, or creating some type of artwork to help them express their feelings and thoughts. A support group for teens or just talking to their friends could be beneficial. If the death was caused by an accident, perhaps they could rally together with other teens to stop the same situation from happening again. They could put flowers or a sign at the scene of the accident, reminding people to slow down. These are just a few ways that adolescents can express themselves, release some of the pain of losing their loved ones, and realize that they have been heard and that someone cares about them.

Language and Logistics

When a death occurs, a child or an adolescent should be told the individual has died in simple, factual, honest terms that will be understood. Using terms such as *passed on* or *passed away* can cause confusion about what really happened. Death is final, not temporary, and children and teens will not be able to visit their loved ones again. Accurate-but-gentle terminology will benefit everyone. Don't use such phrases as "They are asleep and at peace now"; a young child may think that when they go to sleep, they will die too.

The attendance or nonattendance of children at the visitation, funeral, and burial is a frequent concern of parents when a death occurs. If the child wants to go, please allow them to go. Explain in age-appropriate terms what the different services are for. For example, you could explain that the visitation or wake is an opportunity for people to express their sympathies to your family. Tell the child that there may be people there you don't know who knew your loved one, and there might be people who are your friends who will come and say they are sorry that your loved one died. Explain why so many people are crying or laughing: they are sad, but they also remember happy things about your loved one.

It might be a good idea to go the funeral home early, before everyone else gets there, so the child will have time to ask questions and have you answer them without being rushed. If the visitation includes an open casket, explain what the child will see: the body of their loved one. Explain why the body feels cold and hard. If the person was cremated, explain the urn.

Ask the funeral home personnel if they have a place that would be available for children to color or read during the visitation; this allows children to be present but not constantly in the activity of the visitation process. Be sure to check on them throughout the evening if they stay, and have a plan in place in case they want or need to go home early. If they are not attending the funeral, help them say their final goodbyes to their loved ones.

The funeral is a service during which someone speaks about your loved one and provides words of comfort. You remember their lives and what they meant to you. The burial is the conclusion of these remembrance ceremonies. Children may want to go only to the visitation and not the funeral; that is okay too. The purpose behind these activities is to say goodbye. Be sure that when your child leaves, they know that they won't see the deceased loved one again.

For children and teens, grieving may look different than grieving in adults, but it is no less valid or important. Listening to them, caring for them, being honest with them, letting them feel what they feel, and understanding their frustrations and sorrows will allow them to process their grief in a healthy way.

Chapter References

*Kubler-Ross, E., & Kessler, D. (2005). *On grief and grieving.* New York: Scribner.

*Plopper, B. L., & Ness, M. E. (1993). Death as portrayed to adolescents through Top 40 rock and roll music, *Journal on Adolescence 28,* 793–807.

Plumley, R. P. (2007). When a teen is grieving. *One Caring Place.* Indiana: Abbey Press.

*Rathkey, J. W. (2004). *What children need when they grieve.* New York: Three Rivers Press.

* See Annotated References for a short description of this resource.

CHAPTER 4

Sibling Grief

The death of a sibling can have a profound impact on a person's life. Losing a brother or sister in childhood is one of the most confusing and life-changing events a person can experience, second only to losing a parent at a young age. The sibling relationship brings unique aspects to grief, and it's important to remember that the loss is real and deeply felt. The most important thing to remember is that siblings, too, need to feel they have been heard and understood as they navigate through their grief.

Sibling Grief in Childhood

When a young child dies, it is important that children are reassured that they themselves will be okay and that they are safe. They also need to know that they are not at fault and not responsible for a death because they had an argument, fight, or angry words with their sibling in the days before he or she died. Surviving children need to know they are still loved by their families, especially when everyone around them is so overwhelmed by the death.

Often, parents who are dealing with their own grief and who are tired, confused, and maybe even angry, have a hard time dealing with the "normal" childlike questions and activities of their surviving children. Parents may become short-tempered, cry a lot, withdraw from their normal activities, or become overinvolved in activities that don't include their families—and the surviving child or children, who might not understand this change in the family, may feel lost, unloved, or blamed.

Bereaved siblings need to be loved and supported; they need to be allowed to grieve, and they need to have their grief recognized and embraced. This is true both immediately after their siblings have died and through the years of their childhood and teen years. Just as the child who died will always be a part of their parents' past, their siblings will always have the loss as part of their childhood too. This doesn't have to be negative, however. It's all about how the grieving process is handled and about the honesty with which adults discuss the topic. Open, honest, age-appropriate responses about why a sibling died, speaking the deceased child's name, and including memories of the deceased child will help the surviving children grieve and grow in their understanding.

On the other hand, a lack of communication and treating the subject of their sibling's death as a forbidden topic will likely confuse and frustrate surviving children as they go through different developmental stages. The confused five-year-old child soon becomes the scared nine-year-old who becomes a teen who feels unable to live up to the ideal or memory of his or her deceased sibling. Additionally, the surviving children simply miss their siblings, especially in the years that they need them the most.

Children experience many emotions when a sibling dies; they may regress in certain behaviors or act out in other ways, such as reverting back to thumb-sucking, bed-wetting, disrupting their classrooms at school, yelling, turning inward, or simply wanting to be alone. These things may occur because they are not sure what to do or how to act, and they often will stuff their feelings inside rather than talk with someone.

Here are four typical emotions that children and teens may experience after the death of their siblings:

- Anger: They may feel anger because of the death or the way they were told about it, because life goes on in a normal fashion for others but not for them. They may feel angry for being forgotten, for not being let in to their parents' lives, for being left alone or sent away, or for having to compete with the memory of their deceased sibling, who seems perfect.
- Sad: They may feel sadness because of the loss of a companion or innocence, because of loneliness, or just because of the way things have become for their family.
- Bad (guilt and/or anxiety): They may feel "bad" because of their fears, guilt, self-destructive behaviors, distrust, and for never feeling they were good enough.
- Gladness: They may feel glad because they are survivors, because they carry the memories of their sister or brother with them, because they are living for both of them, appreciation of their lives, and more.

Additionally, children's emotions can also be classified broadly into four I-statements that express more succinctly what they are feeling:

- "I hurt inside." This hurt comes from the vulnerability of being human, from loving, and from missing others; these hurts include anger, sadness, frustration, fear, loneliness, irritability, as well as many other emotions. Their behaviors may change to include crying more often, withdrawing, misbehaving, fearing the dark, seeking attention more than usual, or overeating to fill up the hole of emptiness they may feel inside.
- "I don't understand." Young children are particularly vulnerable to thinking that they are responsible for their siblings' deaths because sometimes they fight, argue, or say other things, such as, "I wish you would go away forever," and then,

their siblings die. This confusing and traumatizing turn of events compounds the depth of their emotions, especially their guilt and feelings of responsibility for the outcome.

Siblings need to be told how their brothers or sisters died, especially as they grow older and begin to ask more questions. If their questions are ignored or followed by long, awkward silences from family, they'll begin to feel as if they are different from others and may even feel alone or separated. They may feel there is no longer room for them at home.

- "I don't belong." The surviving siblings may have lost self-esteem and feel that the children who died were their parents' favorites, and now the survivors can't do anything right in their parents' eyes. They may feel responsibility for the deaths of their siblings, especially if there was an accident where one sibling perished but another survived.
- "I'm not enough." A sibling might have a feeling of displacement due to an addition to the family, such as a newborn or an adopted child. The surviving siblings feels they are not enough to make their parents happy anymore because their parents had to get another child to replace the brother or sister who died.

In families where the surviving children were told they were loved and had their questions answered, most of these problems did not occur.

Teens who experience sibling death may be more at risk for negative behaviors than younger children. This is often disenfranchised grief—meaning, it is not always openly acknowledged or publicly mourned—and creates even more pressure as they deal with the loss of their siblings, the anguish of their parents, and the lack of support from their own peers who don't know what to do or say. Teens often feel an imposed code of silence from family members even if they want to share their pain because they are afraid to upset their families. Isolation from their friends also puts them outside their circles of support.

Other variables that could contribute to sibling responses include the type of death, such as the sudden and unexpected versus a progressive life-threatening illness; the closeness of the siblings; and the family's social climate, meaning that if the family is open about grief and share the loss with the remaining children, these children will feel that it is okay to have feelings and not be afraid to cry or ask questions.

Children and teens have their own special burdens to carry when trying to grieve the deaths of their siblings and often do not resolve their grief until they are on their own as an adult, although some bereaved siblings still struggle with this loss as adults. The following characteristics may be true of sibling death survivors; many of these children will have relationship problems as well as depression and low self-esteem as children, teens, and into adulthood:

The Haunted Child. This child's family does not talk about the death of the sibling. This child has no real opportunity to grieve the loss of their brother or sister, possibly not even until they are out of the home environment or is an adult. This can have a devasting impact on the surviving sibling as they become an adult. The child often becomes confused, angry at their parents for not talking about the deceased sibling, feels an emptiness within, and struggles with the grief and the memories of long ago.

The Overprotected Child. This child is so overprotected by fearful parents that it interferes with the child's sense of self-reliance and independence. These overprotected children are also affected in adulthood as their parents' fears are passed on to them and perhaps even on to their grandchildren.

The Lap Child. This child's sibling had been sick for a very long time before his or her death. The sick child has been kept very close to home and has received a great deal of attention. This could very easily cause a sense of passiveness and helplessness in the surviving sibling, who may feel as though they too, must be sick to receive attention.

The Replacement Child. This child either could have been born or adopted after their sibling's death, and then is treated as a replacement for the deceased brother or sister. This child may also struggle in life because of the treatment they receive, such as being ignored or not given the love and attention they should receive from the family. This child may feel they are not able to live up to the deceased sibling, may have low self-esteem, and may have a great deal of problems with relationships in the future.

The Lonely Child. This child is either neglected while their sibling is dying or while everyone is grieving the death of the deceased child, causing the lonely child to grow up feeling like they are an only child. The healthy sibling feels alone and that no one really cares about them because all the family's love and attention is being put onto the dying sibling. Surviving children often grow up resenting the dying child as well as their families.

The Later-Born Child. This child is born into the family after the death of the deceased child and may feel resentment that they never had the chance to know the deceased brother or sister. A later-born child may see the deceased brother or sister as a guardian angel or may even resent the deceased child for dying and for making their parents sad or overprotective.

The Scapegoat Child. This child bears the brunt of the family's unhappiness and frequent hostility brought on by the guilt and regret of the deceased sibling. Scapegoat children often feel that they could never live up to their deceased siblings no matter what they accomplish in life. They may feel that no matter what they do, it will never be enough to equal their deceased siblings or ever bring happiness back to the family. These children will often have relationship problems in the future as they seek someone who will give them love and acceptance and who will accept them as they are.

Adult Sibling Grief

Sibling death in adulthood has its own facets of grief, especially in the prime-of-life years. Older adults grieve strongly after the deaths of their siblings, as they lose their lifelong companions. Age, circumstances, and the strength—or lack thereof—of sibling bonds all contribute to the grieving process.

From childhood to adulthood, siblings tend to go their separate ways. Some siblings maintain strong bonds through adulthood, while others aren't as strong but are nevertheless congenial. Some siblings may grow apart for a variety of reasons as they become adults; the familial bond that ties siblings together emotionally usually means that what happens to one sibling will have an impact on the whole family no matter how far away they live or how strained their relationships are at the time.

The death of an adult sibling can also be very devastating. It really is the epitome of disenfranchised grief. It can be a loss that is not really acknowledged or mourned publicly by society as perhaps a child, spouse, or parent would be. I still remember when my brother died suddenly from a stroke and how difficult that was for me. The effect of this loss depends a great deal on how close the relationship was before the death, as well as how close the siblings were in childhood and how many life experiences they shared. It may also bring up good memories of their childhood and memories of conflicts and sibling rivalry. Childhood resentments against the deceased sibling may come up; it is important to deal with them and not let them fester.

As with any type of grief, the impact of sibling bereavement often lasts a lifetime. Many years following the death of a sibling, bereaved siblings often experience renewed and intense grief on special occasions such as graduations, weddings, births, challenges in their careers, and even in retirement. The main advice from grieving siblings to their families is: Don't forget that we are hurting too. Please listen to us, love us, show us you care, and don't forget about us.

Chapter References

Alberta Foundation for Nursing Research (1985). Behavioral responses of children to the death of a sibling (Final report). Edmonton, Alberta: B. Davies.

*Brett, M., & Davis, E. M. B. (1998). What does it mean? Sibling and parental appraisals of childhood leukemia. *Cancer Nursing 11*, 329–338.

Davies, B. (1999). *Shadows in the sun: Experiences of sibling bereavement in childhood.* Philadelphia: Brunner-Mozel.

Dyregrov, K., & Dyregrov, A. (2005). Helping the family following suicide. In B. Monroe & F. Kraus (Eds.), *Brief interventions with bereaved children* (pp. xxx–xxx). Oxford: Oxford University Press.

Phillips, S. (2013). Do we recognize the grief of losing a sibling? *University of Phoenix: WGBH Educational Foundation & Vulcan Productions Inc.*

White, P. G. (2006). *Sibling grief: Healing after the death of a sister or brother.* Lincoln, NE: I Universe.

* See Annotated References for a short description of this resource

CHAPTER 5

Grief and Those Who Have Developmental Disabilities

Often those with developmental disabilities are forgotten, and no one really talks about them or how to help them when a death occurs. The term *developmental disabilities* refers to a severe, chronic disability of a person who is five years old or older, such as those with Down Syndrome, autism, cerebral palsy, or any other cognitive impairment. It refers to individuals who have an IQ below seventy and who typically learn and develop mentally slower than others.

This is an example of a family with a teenage son who has a developmental disability and how the family handled the death of his grandfather. The family struggled with whether or not to tell the boy, who had autism, that his grandfather had died. This young man was very intelligent, but he could become violent when provoked or confused. They thought about not telling him, but then decided to talk with him. He was close to his grandparents, and his family was afraid that if they did not tell him his grandfather had died, he surely would wonder and ask why his grandpa was not coming around to see him anymore and why the family seemed so sad all the time. They waited a couple days and then spoke with him. His family said he took the news very hard but seemed to understand what was being said.

A person with developmental disabilities can have an especially difficult time understanding when someone dies, particularly when the deceased is someone they know and love. Some families or caregivers think that these individuals will not feel or understand (or are not capable of feeling or understanding) the loss and should be protected from the truth. However, as previously mentioned, by not talking about or acknowledging the loss, the individual could have a more difficult time when the person who has died does not come to see them anymore.

Another concern for families and caregivers is how their family members with developmental disabilities will respond when a loss or death occurs. Like anyone else who experiences a loss, an individual with a developmental, social, or emotional disability may also experience changes in their sleeping patterns and eating habits, withdrawing or being overly active, or even suffering possible severe physical symptoms and personality changes. However, the difficulty lies in the possibility, or even the likelihood, that their caregivers and family members may not know how to console them or help them cope because their reactions to this confusing and upsetting situation may be outside the caregiver's comfort zone or knowledge—repetitive actions with nonsense words, loud crying, or other physical or verbal reactions that may seem excessively loud or embarrassing.

It is also very possible that these individuals may deal with a lack of social support, as it is not uncommon for individuals with developmental, emotional, or social disabilities to be marginalized and left out of many social settings.

Losing a loved one creates a cycle of change for anyone. For individuals with disabilities, losing their primary caregivers, especially if they are their parents, can be extremely difficult to cope with all the ensuing changes. Other losses, such as living arrangements, daily routines, attention and support, and financial stability could happen in quick succession after the death of a caregiver. This type of situation can be extremely unsettling and scary. The future may seem bleak and uncertain to these individuals, and they may fear what could be awaiting them next.

How can we help these bereaved individuals? Here are five important actions that will help them cope:

1. **Tell the person about the death.** If the person is not informed, they may wonder why their parent, friend, or caregiver has stopped visiting and may feel they did something wrong to cause this. The more direct and immediate the knowledge about the loss, the less disbelief is likely to come into play. Being compassionate and honest are the best first steps to take.
2. **Encourage and allow the person to share their feelings.** This might cause the family to be uncomfortable, but it is vital that these individuals are allowed to feel what they feel.
3. **Reassure the bereaved individual they are not alone.** Others are there to help.
4. **Be patient as they grieve.** They should not be rushed in their grief. It is very important for them to be able to tell and retell stories about the people who died as well as share details about the deceased's illness and death. This telling and retelling helps the bereaved to hear and accept the reality of what happened and to adjust to this new reality.
5. **Listen to the bereaved.** Learn from them so they can be helped both now and in the future.

Warning Signs/Complicating Factors

Understanding, problem-solving, processing facts, and planning next steps are activities that developmentally, socially, and mentally disabled people may have difficulty with, even without the added stress of grief. Some warning signs and complicating factors to be aware of include:

1. **Experiencing overload due to multiple losses.** Multiple losses could be the deaths of more than one friend or relative, either in the same incident or in quick succession of each other. It could also be the result of one person's death, but that event leads to significant changes as a result, such as where will the disabled person live? Who will take care of their finances? What will the individual's new community be like? Who will be there for support?
2. **Idolizing the deceased.** It is important to talk about the positive and negative aspects of the deceased person's habits and personality and not dwell only on the positive aspects of the deceased. Sometimes the individual has become so attached to the person who died they tend to idolize (put the deceased on a pedestal—it is as if the person could do no wrong).
3. **Acting out in harmful or inappropriate ways, such as throwing things, having a temper tantrum, yelling out.**
4. **Using alcohol or drugs excessively and not realizing just how easily this could lead to addictions.**
5. **Talking about suicide after a death has occurred.** This is not unusual among the bereaved, but it could be a warning sign that family or caregivers should talk with the individual and assess their mental and emotional state.
6. **Developing the physical symptoms of the deceased.** This should be checked out by a physician and not ignored or left to get worse. In other words, the person could begin to have chest pains, severe headaches like migraines, dizziness, trouble breathing, or aches and pains that they never had before. These may be real symptoms or can be psychosomatic, but they should never be ignored.
7. **Experiencing extreme sleep deprivation.** Sleeplessness is a typical part of normal grief, but if it becomes extreme, it could have even more physical repercussions for the bereaved.
8. **Having a difficult relationship with the deceased in the past.** If the relationship between the bereaved and the deceased

was strained or broken, the fact that it cannot be repaired or improved may cause an intensely emotional response or feeling of guilt for the bereaved. Alternatively, it may be that the bereaved and the deceased had little or no interaction at all, so the death is not traumatic in the sense of loss but rather in the sense of ambivalence and disinterest.

9. **Experiencing a loss with a stigma.** A sudden, unexpected, or stigmatized death, such as an accident, a homicide, AIDS, or suicide, can cause even more confusion and complications for a person with developmental challenges.

Several strategies can help those with developmental disabilities understand better. For example, tell the truth about the death of a loved one using several small steps—short sentences and simple words. People with developmental disabilities are often visual and/or kinesthetic learners, so visual aids, such as a picture of the person who died, are recommended when explaining about a loved one's death. If the individual wants to go to the visitation or funeral, explain before they go what they could possibly see and hear, especially what the deceased loved one will look like and feel like if touched. Explain what the casket or urn is. Explain the different parts of the service. If the casket is open, explain that, at the end of the service, there will be a time to say goodbye and then the casket will be closed. Be ready to give the individual answers right away because they need instant feedback. This will help the person with their behavior as well as their questions.

It would be a good idea to take the individual to the visitation or funeral before everyone else arrives so that they can spend some private time with the deceased loved one and you can answer questions, and the individual won't have to feel that everyone is staring at them. It might be very difficult for the person to stay. Having a place to go after the indiviudal sees their loved one might be a good idea. The person should not be left alone with the deceased in case the whole experience becomes too much. The individual may want to leave or may be afraid to go up to the casket; or they may try to get into the casket or try to get the deceased out of the casket because they does not understand the deceased is truly dead. At the funeral or after the death, never tell the bereaved that the deceased is sleeping or has passed away or that the deceased "is in heaven with Jesus or God," because the bereaved may want to go see the deceased and bring them back without understanding that it's not possible.

If family and friends take their time explaining everything slowly and truthfully to individuals with developmental disabilities or delays about their loved ones' deaths and what they may see and hear at the visitation or funeral, the experience will be less traumatic for them as they struggle with the loss of their loved ones.

Chapter References

*Bowlby, J. (1980). *Attachment and loss: Loss, sadness and depression.* New York: Basic Books.

Cook, A. S., & Dworkin, D. S. (1992). *Helping the bereaved: Therapeutic interventions for children, adolescents and adults.* New York: Basic Books.

Kloeppel, D. A. & Hollis, S. (1989). Double handicap: Mental retardation and death in the family. *Death Studies, 13,* 31–38.

Luchterhand, C., & Murphy, N. (1998). *Helping adults with mental retardation grieve a death loss.* Bristol, PA: Accelerated Development.

*Rando, T. (1993). *The treatment of complicated mourning.* Champaign, IL: Research Press.

*Worden, J. W. (2002). *Grief counseling and grief therapy: A handbook for the mental health practitioner* (3rd ed.). New York: Springer.

* See Annotated References for a short description of this resource.

CHAPTER 6

The Death of a Pet and Pets Grieve Too

The death of a pet is something that happens to all pet owners, yet so many of them are embarrassed to grieve this loss. Many people, especially those who do not have or like animals, think grieving the loss of an animal is absolutely ridiculous and a waste of time and energy.

"It's only an animal; it's not a human," people say. But in a sense, we do humanize our pets. We invite them into our lives, our families, our joys, and our sorrows. We talk to them, cuddle them, and discipline them as needed. We feed them, give them their favorite treats and toys, and take them to the vet to ensure their health and well-being. Pets may know more about us than most of our families or friends do—either because we've told them our deepest secrets or they've observed our habits and reactions for so long, or, most likely, both—and they still love us unconditionally. Their love for us is everlasting. Their main job and goal in life is to love us and please us—no matter what. On those sad, lonely, sick days, they will be by our sides to love us and sit with us quietly. They are there to greet us when we come home.

Whether our beloved pets are dogs, cats, birds, gerbils, or goldfish, they become part of our families. A pet can be a companion, a confidant, a friend, a good listener, a protector, an emotional support, or and exercise partner—plus they give us unconditional love. Animals can help lower our stress levels as well as our blood pressure.

In our society, we are expected to downplay our grief over the death of a pet because our grief often lingers on long after the loss has occurred. I am one of those people who grieved the death of my pets. People who knew me knew my beagles, Dirky and Max, as well. My first beagle was a stray that I named Dirky because I found her on Dirksen Parkway, a very busy road with many businesses along the street. We went everywhere together—to the bank, to look for a new car, to get a Christmas tree—even to the store. After she died in 1997, it took ten years before I was emotionally ready to look for another dog. Max was a rescue who came with his name. He came into my life in 2007. He and I went everywhere together as well. Max was always there to comfort me on difficult days and to rejoice with me on happy days. He loved to play ball, run, go for walks, and ride in the car, but he was scared of storms. He even had a special friend at the bank who always gave him more treats than anyone else. Max died on Wednesday, May 15, 2019.

After the dogs died, I buried them in the backyard in special places marked off just for them. Our normal routines were difficult for a while. It was strange to go to the bank and see the box of dog biscuits in the window but realize no treats would be included in the tube with my deposit receipt, or to look for a Christmas tree or go for walks with my neighbor and her beagle, Willie, without Max. I still miss them very much.

In most instances, the human will outlive the pet, so it's important to realize from the outset that the likelihood of having to say goodbye is quite high. When considering the lifespan of a pet and how that fits within the timeframe of your care, it's important to remember that there will be at least three very significant days in your relationship. The first is the day you bring your pet home—a day of happiness, excitement, and anticipation of what life will be like as you fall into a routine together. The second day occurs about eight or nine years later, when you look at your pet and see age instead of youth. You notice a slower pace instead of frenetic energy. You may even feel a gnawing anticipation that someday, though hopefully not soon, your pet will no longer be a part of your life. When the third day comes, you may be faced with making a heart-wrenching decision on your pet's behalf—or you may simply find your pet has died in the night. In whatever manner your pet leaves you, it will likely be one of the loneliest and saddest days of your life.

"If you are wise," states Martin Scot Kosins, a pet lover who wrote of his grief, "you will let the tears flow as freely and as often as they must. If you are typical, you will find that many in your circle of family or friends will not be able to understand your grief or comfort you. This loss, like any other loss in your life, is not something that you will 'get over'—but rather with time you will 'get through it.' So, love your animals and protect them while you can for that third day will arrive someday."

It is natural to feel overwhelmed with feelings of grief and sadness when your pet dies. Though others may not understand the depth of your feelings, it is not about what they think; it's about you and your pet. Many people think of a cat or dog as *just* a cat or dog, but pets are beloved members of a family, and when they die, their loss is significant. Usually, the level of grief depends on several factors, such as the age of the pet (was the pet young or old), the personality of the pet (what was the pet really like; what made him or her so special to you?) and how the pet died. Did the pet die suddenly from an unexpected tumor or disease or accident, or did your pet go through many weeks or months of being sick and then die?

Everyone grieves differently because grief is a personal experience. Losing a pet may not be exactly the same as losing a spouse, family member, or close friend, but the grief is still very real. As such, keep these four things in mind: (1) The grieving process happens a little at a time, so be patient with yourself. (2) It is okay to feel what you feel when your pet dies—don't let others make you feel embarrassed. (3) Don't ignore your pain—face your pain and deal with it, as difficult as that might be. (4) Don't ever apologize for how you feel.

Remember that not everyone loves your pet or even animals in general, so don't expect all your friends and relatives to rally around you when your pet dies. If you accept the fact that not everyone loves animals, it's easier to avoid arguing with someone about how they or you feel. More importantly, surround yourself with positive animal lovers who will both sympathize and empathize with your loss.

Lawrence Robinson, Jeanne Segal, and Robert Segal, in their book *Coping with Pet Loss*, suggest these six healthy ways of coping with grief after the death of a pet:

1. Don't let anyone ever tell you how you should feel. Feel what you feel and don't feel embarrassed about it.
2. Reach out to others whose pets have died. Seek out a grief support group or start your own.
3. Have a funeral or gathering—whatever helps you get through the pain of your loss.
4. Create a legacy in memory of your pet: designate a memorial, plant a tree, make a scrapbook in memory of your pet, or donate money to an animal shelter in your pet's name.
5. Take care of yourself mentally, physically, and emotionally. Be sure to eat healthy and get some sleep as well as some exercise.
6. If there are other pets in the home, maintain their normal routines as much as possible.

Older adults often have pets as their companions; when their companions die, it is usually devastating for them because this relationship is so very important to them. Their pets often are what keep them going in their lives. Caregivers and family should take this loss seriously and reach out to these older adults to help them cope with the death of their pets. Family and friends should continue to support and to listen to them. It is also important in this situation for the elderly to eat, sleep, and get some exercise so as to give them the energy they need to get through each day and deal with the loss.

Another concern for older adults is the question of what will happen to their beloved pets when they die—who will be there to take care of them? Will someone in the family take care of the pet? Will the pet have to be taken to a shelter? These are questions that should be answered for older adults to give them some peace of mind.

Children also experience grief and pain when their pets die. The loss of a pet is often a child's first experience with death. How this experience is handled by family and friends could shape their thought process and life forever. It is essential to be honest with children and not use metaphors, euphemisms, or clichés to explain their pets' deaths. For example, don't tell them their pets ran away if they really died. It is much healthier for the family and for children if they have a ritual for saying goodbye to their pets, instead of looking all over the neighborhood for a pet that had already died.

Some people do not understand the importance of a close attachment with a pet. And because of this, certain attitudes could lead to well-intended actions taken by family members that could cause the bereavement experience to become more difficult. In the book *The Accident* by Carol Carrick, a dog is hit by a truck and killed while the child is at school. The family buries the dog to spare the little boy the sadness of burying his dog. However, the family does not realize the harm they are causing by leaving him out of this sad-but-necessary ritual.

The child grieves and feels the pain as others who experience the death of a pet do, so it is important for the family to listen to the child's feelings and allow them to process these emotions. Don't try to make the child feel better by rushing out and buying another animal. Assure the child that you will be around to listen whenever they feel like talking about this death (a wonderful teaching moment to explain about death, especially because this could be the first death for a child). If the pet is very sick and the decision has been made to euthanize it, please allow the child to say goodbye first. Tell the child the truth and explain what happened to their pet and what will happen next. It would be a good idea to have your veterinarian talk to the child to explain what is happening and what can or cannot be done to help the pet.

Loss and grief are also very evident when someone realizes they can no longer care for a pet and must give it away to someone else to care for it. It is a difficult decision but one that must be made sometimes. In these situations, if it is possible, make sure the pet goes to a loving, caring new owner or family that can help mitigate the feelings of loss: if the pet can't be with a child, at least they know it's being loved and cared for in its new home.

Losing and grieving a pet can teach many lessons that we would do well to remember in all loss situations. It shows us the importance of relationship and that it's more than just who the relationship is with. It teaches situational importance in that the cause of death and the way death happened can affect the bereavement process. And it especially highlights the importance of the bereaved—friends and family can learn to understand the pain and sadness the bereaved experience after the loss of a pet.

Pet Grief

We know that most people grieve the death of a pet, but do animals themselves grieve the loss of their human companions? The answer is *yes*, pets do grieve. They even show signs of sadness and some depression. The most obvious evidence of pet grief is a loss of appetite and withdrawal or frequent revisiting of places that had meaning for them. Pets may also show grief by sitting by or on a chair where their now deceased owner always sat, or by returning to their owner's gravesite for days or weeks after the death. They also cling to the bereaved to help care for and support them in their grief.

Animals may also grieve the death of other animals. The American Society for the Prevention of Cruelty to Animals (ASPCA) in 1996 conducted a survey to gauge the degree of pet responses to the death of another pet. The survey included observations about eating habits, vocalizations, solicitations of affection, and other activities after the death of a "sibling" animal. Responses showed that more than a third of the dogs in the survey demanded more attention and 25 percent were described as "needy" or "clingy." The responses for cats were slightly different, with almost 40 percent needing more attention, and only 20 percent were characterized as being clingy or needy. Grieving cats are still cats, after all. Another typical response of a grieving pet is the loss or change in appetite for several days up to months at a time. The conclusion of the survey was that, yes, pets show signs of grief. It has also been proven that not only dogs and cats grieve, but ducks, horses, rabbits, and birds do as well.

Even in the wild, animals show grief. One day, I was sitting on my sofa when I heard a loud bang on the patio window. I looked up and saw that a female tufted titmouse bird had flown into the window and was lying on the deck. Within minutes, a male tufted titmouse bird came to her rescue. He pecked and pecked at her as if trying to revive her, but to no avail. A smaller bird appeared, but he shooed it away. The male continued to try to revive her until he realized it was hopeless, at which point he laid his body against the female's for several minutes and then flew away. It was a sad, but beautiful example of an animal showing grief over the death of a loved one.

Remember, if you ever suspect your pet is grieving, be sure to give them that extra attention and unconditional love they so deserve.

Where Does the 'Rainbow Bridge Come From?

The idea of the Rainbow Bridge, and all of its lore, comes from one of several poems written in the 1980s. Several authors claim to have written the original version of "The Rainbow Bridge," and the true origin of the term "Rainbow Bridge" remains unknown.

But one thing is sure: ever since it popped into existence, "The Rainbow Bridge" has inspired and consoled pet owners and pet professionals on a nearly universal level.

Versions of "The Rainbow Bridge"

Just as any work with unknown origins does when it reaches the public, "The Rainbow Bridge" has evolved over time and many different versions of the poem can be found.

The Rainbow Bridge

Just this side of heaven is a place called Rainbow Bridge.

When an animal dies that has been especially close to someone here, that pet goes to Rainbow Bridge.

There are meadows and hills for all of our special friends so they can run and play together.

There is plenty of food, water and sunshine, and our friends are warm and comfortable.

All the animals who had been ill and old are restored to health and vigor; those who were hurt or maimed are made whole and strong again, just as we remember them in our dreams of days and times gone by.

The animals are happy and content, except for one small thing; they each miss someone very special to them, who had to be left behind.

They all run and play together, but the day comes when one suddenly stops and looks into the distance. His bright eyes are intent; His eager body quivers.

Suddenly he begins to run from the group, flying over the green grass, his legs carrying him faster and faster.

You have been spotted, and when you and your special friend finally meet, you cling together in joyous reunion, never to be parted again. The happy kisses rain upon your face; your hands again caress the beloved head, and you look once more into the trusting eyes of your pet, so long gone from your life but never absent from your heart.

Then you cross Rainbow Bridge together...

Chaper References

Adamec, C. (2000). *When your pet dies: Dealing with your grief and helping your children cope.* Lincoln, NE: iUniverse.

Hageman, W. (2013). Pets grieve too. *Tribune Newspaper,* 1–3.

King, B. (2013). *How animals grieve.* Chicago: University of Chicago Press.

Kosins, M. S. (1996). *Maya's first rose: diary of a very special love.* New York, Routledge.

Lagoni, L., Butler, C., & Hett, S. (1994). *The human–animal bond and grief.* Philadelphia: W. B. Saunders.

Palmer, B. (2009). Will your dog mourn your death? *The Washington Post,* pp.1–7.

Robinson, L., Segal, J., & Segal, R. (2013). Coping with Pet Loss. Help guide for ages 1–6. https://www.helpguide.org/articles/grief/coping-with-losing-a-pet.htm.

*Robinson, L., Segal J., & Segal, R. (2013). Coping with Pet Loss: Grieving the death of a dog or cat and moving on. https://www.helpguide.org/articles/grief/coping-with-losing-a-pet.htm.

Rynearson, E. K. (1978). *Humans and pets and attachments, 133*: 550–555.

Stewart, M. F. (1999). *Companion animal deaths: A practical and comprehensive guide for veterinary practice.* Woburn, MA: Butterworth-Hernemann Medical.

Carrick,C. (1984). *The Accident,* Clarion Books.New York: Seabury Press.

* See Annotated References for a short description of this resource.

CHAPTER 7

Grief of Family and Friends of Those Who Have Died by Suicide

The question that survivors of a loved one's suicide ask and rarely get an answer that satisfies, is *why?* Why would someone voluntarily and intentionally end their own life? Unfortunately, a completed suicide often leaves surviving family and friends at a loss when trying to understand and move through the grieving process. Because suicide is a voluntary and intentional act, it has additional emotional elements that death due to accident, illness, or old age do not carry. Being the survivor of a loved one's suicide brings about many intense emotions in addition to the feelings of sadness and loss: guilt, anger, shame, and frustration magnify the perceived—and sadly, sometimes real—stigma connected to a suicide.

What is *guilt?* It is simply anger that has turned inward. Survivors feel as though they should have recognized their loved ones' pain and tried to help them more—even if they had, in fact, already helped their loved ones deal with their issues. They feel that, if they had only listened more, reached out to them more, and judged less, their loved ones would be alive today.

Guilt is normal for families and friends to experience because, no matter what anyone says, they feel they should have recognized the warning signs of their loved ones' suicides and taken them more seriously. What survivors need to understand is, their loved ones' suicides are not their fault. They cannot and should not place blame on themselves.

A survivor's intense anger stems from their inability to understand the depth of pain their loved one experienced to the point of not being able to reach out to anyone else for help before choosing to take their life. Survivors may simply be angry at their loved ones for making what seems to have been a selfish decision. Anger can also be directed at the "system"—for example, if the doctor had prescribed the right medicine, or if the deceased had found a better counselor, if only, if only. Again, anger is not uncommon, but it can be misplaced.

Shame signifies humiliation or reproach, as if others are judging the deceased and the family by assuming negative and often untrue ideas of this family's life and dynamics that would drive someone to do such a thing to him or herself and family. The stigma, or the "mark" of shame—not necessarily an outward, physical mark in modern society but rather that of reputation, gossip, or judgment—of a suicide is very real and alive today. Examples include instances where people will cross the street rather than talk to someone whose family member has died by suicide, or bereaved individuals who lie to their friends rather than tell them that a loved one died from suicide because they fear potential rejection, loss of friendships, or malicious gossip. They are afraid of what others may think of them because "suicide doesn't happen in stable families" or because "something should have been done to stop it"—or so some would like to believe. Unfortunately, others don't always realize the truth unless they have been through it themselves. Some people, especially if they have a strong faith background, feel ashamed because they worry that others might judge their level of faith or somehow assume there is hidden sin in their lives. There is even a fear that certain clergy will not bury their loved ones if the death is a suicide.

It is any wonder that bereaved survivors feel abandoned not only by their loved ones who died by suicide but also by their families and friends? They may feel isolated and cut off from everyone around them. Survivors may feel betrayed because their own parent or child or spouse or sibling completed a suicide and didn't try to talk with them about what they were feeling about or the struggles they were facing. They may feel intense frustration because, had they known of their loved ones' struggles, perhaps they could have helped in whatever ways they could to support and encourage them to seek counseling, medications, therapy, rehab—anything to prevent exactly what ended up happening anyway. This frustration leads to a loss of trust for the bereaved who feels betrayed by their loved ones because, before the death, they felt they knew everything about their deceased loved ones, but now they question what else they didn't know.

Many families wish their loved ones would have written a note or letter or somehow left an explanation to help explain why they ended their lives. Often, if there is a note or message of some kind, it doesn't provide an explanation but rather a means of saying goodbye and asking for the family's forgiveness. Finding a note does not always answer the question *why*. In the long run, it could cause the bereaved even more frustration that they did not get a specific answer to their question.

The shock of a suicide forces the survivors to reevaluate and relive the past to search for answers, but the *should have's* and *could have's* serve only to compound their guilt. It's hard to accept that a loved one saw no other way out of their pain than to end their life. Yet, what is so hard for the survivors to remember is that *their loved ones' suicides are not their fault*.

Why do people choose to take their lives? The main reason is overwhelming pain—but whether it is physical, mental, emotional, spiritual, or social makes no difference. Dr. Edwin S. Shneidman spent most of his life studying suicide and came to this conclusion: Suicide is caused by *psychache*. This term describes the insurmountable mental pain caused by the frustration and lack of fulfillment of an individual's most important, unique needs. He goes on to list four categories of these needs: (1) thwarted love, acceptance, or belonging; (2) fractured control, helplessness, and frustration; (3) assaulted self-image and avoidance of shame, defeat, humiliation, and disgrace; and (4) ruptured key relationships and attendant grief and bereavement.

The pain that goes with the feelings of hopelessness and helplessness and the feeling that there is no way out of the situation creates a tunnel vision, in which the only conclusion they can see is to end their part in these struggles—if they don't exist, their struggles and frustrations will cease to exist as well. Therefore, they cannot feel the love around them or feel those who are reaching out to them; they feel only the pain that is within them that is driving them in the direction they feel they need to go.

It's important to note there is a difference between someone who thinks about a suicide and someone who actually ends their life. The person who thinks about ending their life but doesn't has not lost all hope in their future and is able to pull back and recover a normal, balanced sense of life before it is too late. However, the person who actually ends their life sees no way out of the pain and sees no hope in the future. People who have a plan to end their lives are very good at covering it up so that no one can stop them from completing their plans. Once they make the decision to end their lives, their whole demeanor changes and they seem very happy. This false sense of security provides relief to everyone else, which then frees the person to execute their plan.

Often, there is a pattern or path of this hopelessness, helplessness, or depression that has developed over many months or even years and that can be traced to an earlier time in their lives. This information can be helpful to families to perhaps help the rest of their family in the future, especially if they feel another family member seems depressed or anxious. When a bereaved person feels abandoned and unable to deal with their emotions or life without the deceased person and feels a strong desire to be with their loved one, the bereaved may want to end their life too. Love and support from the family and friends of these partners is crucial in these situations.

Helping Those Who Grieve Suicide

One very important element of the healing process after a completed suicide is forgiveness—forgiving your loved one *and* yourself. Survivors must come to understand that their loved ones were in so much pain, they could not ask for help because they felt they were alone and that no one would be able to understand what they felt. Even if you were very close to the person who died by suicide, they still would not have been able to reach out to you and ask for help at the end because of tunnel vision. In the deceased's mind, this person carried the weight of the world on their shoulders.

How do you forgive yourself for your anger and guilt when really, there was nothing you could have done to save or stop someone? You can forgive yourself because your loved one's suicide was not your fault.

How do you forgive your loved one? You eventually come to a place of understanding their feelings of hopelessness and helplessness—the person's psychache—was too overwhelming for their mind to turn back. If you can accept the idea that the deceased's anguish was to blame, not they themselves, for the inability to ask family and friends for help, you can forgive them. When you can remember the good in the person's life instead of its tragic end, you are forgiving the deceased. As with all types of grief, this process takes time. It might take more effort with a suicide, but in the end, the act of forgiving yourself and your loved one will free both of you from unrealized expectations and unfounded blame.

Suicide is very complicated; it's difficult for families and friends to understand why someone would not only attempt a suicide but actually complete one without realizing that it's not a temporary fix to a problem, but rather a sad permanent solution.

How can we help the bereaved? Here are several suggestions:

- Acknowledge their pain, but don't try to take it away from them; they must go through grief to heal.
- Be sensitive to their needs and allow them to cry if they need to.

- Give them permission to feel what they feel, and don't tell them that everything will be okay.
- Mention their loved ones' names and encourage them to do the same.
- Listen deeply to them; allow them to be heard; do not give them advice, but rather, allow them to tell their stories over and over again.
- Don't judge or criticize them or their loved ones.
- Don't make them feel that they need to apologize for how they feel; accept them where they are.
- Call them, bring food by, but not in a disposable container—that way, you will have to go back to get it and can see them again.
- Do not expect them to be further along in their grief simply because it is uncomfortable for *you* to see them in so much pain.
- Go for a walk or out to eat with the bereaved and *listen* to them.

It can be very helpful for the bereaved to attend a suicide support group, as well as seek counseling with a grief therapist or mental health counselor to help them talk about the pain they are feeling after their loved ones' suicides. It is very important for the bereaved of any type of loss to establish a connection of trust, security, and overall rapport with a therapist before they actually get too far into their therapy sessions. If they feel there is no connection, it would be better to seek a new therapist than to waste their time and money with someone they feel cannot help them.

Sometimes medications may be necessary to "take the edge off" and help with anxiety, depression, as well as sleeplessness; however, as with any medication, be aware that some side effects can cause problems as well.

Support and being heard—being able and being encouraged to express raw feelings and process emotions in their own timing—is very important for anyone who experiences the death of a family member or friend through suicide. The following information is included to help with recognizing signs for teen and older adult suicide.

Teen Suicide

When teens contemplates suicide, they may use direct or indirect threats about their thought processes. A direct threat is simple and to the point: "I'm going to kill myself" or "By next week I'll be dead" or "I'm going to blow my brains out." These threats should be taken seriously and never ignored. An indirect threat is not as easy to recognize as a direct threat because it uses more causal language: "I wish I were dead" or "You'd be better off without me" or "I can't do anything right." Regardless of whether it is direct or indirect, pay attention and don't disregard the comment as a mood. It could be; but it could be more serious.

Suicidal Signs in Teens:

- Sudden changes in behavior, such as eating too much or not wanting to eat; sleeping late or not sleeping enough; changes in their schoolwork and attendance; changes in their appearance and cleanliness; withdrawal from activities and friends; turning inward. This could go on for several days or weeks before they actually complete a suicide.
- Significant losses, including struggling to understand or accept the recent death of a significant person in their lives.
- Giving away treasured possessions, giving away their clothes, collections, or other possessions, saying, "I won't be needing these."
- Tying-up loose ends or resolving unfinished business, such as repaying a loan, answering a letter they have been putting off, or returning something borrowed.
- Aggression, rebellion, and disobedience, such as expressing anger at friends, parents, teachers, and coaches—someone who

has hurt or disappointed them in some way. Teens may act out or even become hostile, which could distance them from the people who can help them.
- Self-destructive behaviors, such as smoking, drinking, abusing drugs, or driving their bikes and cars recklessly.
- Loss of self-esteem: feeling as though they are ugly, dumb, unimportant, or insignificant. They feel lost, like they don't fit in anymore, can't seem to do anything right, and that no one cares about them or loves them. Teens who break up with their significant others may also feel life is not worth living anymore because they feel betrayed or want to punish the ones who are left behind.

It is very important for friends, parents, family, teachers, and coaches to be aware of these warning signs and to act on them. Teens will not present all of these signs or may try to hide them, so it is important to be aware of each one before some kind of action takes place.

Suicidal teens need:

- Someone who will talk with them face-to-face and be honest with them.
- Someone who will listen to and help them to feel they have been heard.
- Someone who will help them understand that it is okay to feel what they are feeling so they can better understand what is going on inside of them.
- Someone who will be there for them, someone they can depend on—a caring friend.

Teens and young adults who are using medications for bipolar disorder or other chemical imbalances sometimes stop taking their medications because they feel better. Unfortunately, the lack of necessary medications in their systems can cause them to experience depression and hopelessness, leading them to end their lives. There are also those who want revenge against someone who hurt them or who would not let them play in a sports activity or who abused them in some manner. Teens often do not realize that suicide is a permanent fix, one in which they cannot go back to see the reactions of the ones they left behind. There are also those who experience accidental suicides from playing with guns, drugs, or alcohol. Although they did not plan to take their lives, they thought it would be fun to experiment and perhaps get high, with tragic results.

Older Adult Suicides:

The older generation is very often overlooked, and when they lose their spouses, their health deteriorates without hope of improvement, or they simply become depressed about how their lives have turned out, they may choose to end their lives, taking their families and friends completely by surprise. Their families are forced to deal with the stigma of suicide that is now connected to them and their loved ones, and struggle with the many emotions of guilt, anger, shock, and shame.

Sometimes survivors who have had more than one family member die by suicide will feel that they, too, are destined to the same ending in their own lives. They must realize that suicide does not have to happen to them because it happened to someone in their families. However, because suicidal behaviors are multidimensional and multifaceted, the social and psychological explanations of suicide come together in an integrated fashion.

Many families that have experienced the suicide of a loved one may experience similar emotions, but perhaps not to the same degree. In other words, not all suicides are the same and can't really be compared to one another. For example, in the case of the elderly man who had a great deal of pain and disability from a terminal illness who decided to end his life, his family would certainly experience grief, but on some level, they might also feel some sense of relief that he will no longer be in the physical pain that he was before.

Contrast that with the suicide of a healthy and smart adolescent who had severe depression and a lot of self-doubt. In this case, the young adolescent's family may not understand why or how this could have happened. They may experience a great deal of anger and guilt at themselves and everyone around them, perhaps because they didn't expect their child to end her life and may have felt the teen had his or her depression under control with medication. The family may, however, feel a deep sense of responsibility and remorse for not having prevented the suicide.

These examples show how each death, regardless of the reason, has unique qualities and impacts each family and individual differently. Allowing and encouraging everyone who has been impacted by the suicide of a loved one to express their feelings in open and honest ways to process them and grieve in the way survivors need to is the best course of action.

Chapter References

*Allen, N. H., & Peek, M. L. (1975). *Suicide and young people* [Brochure]. PLACE: American Association of Suicidology.

*Farberow, N. L. (1991). Adult survivors after suicide: Research problems and needs. In A. Leenaars (Ed.), *Life span perspectives of suicide proces.* New York: Plenum.

Harvey, A. D. (1986). Evidence of a tense shift in personal experiences narratives. *Empirical Studies of the Arts 4*(2), 151–162.

Kubler-Ross, E., & Kessler, D. (2005). *On grief and grieving.* New York: Scribner.

Miller, M. (1985). Suicide prevention. Franciscan Medical Center, *Address to Health Care Professionals & Clergy.* Rock Island, Illinois.

*Nelson, R. E., & Galas, J. C. (1994). *The power to prevent suicide.* Minneapolis, MN: Free Spirit Publishing Co.

Shneidman, E. S. (1993). Suicide as psychache. *Journal of Nervous and Mental Diseases, 181*(3), 147–149.

* See Annotated References for a short description of this resource.

CHAPTER 8

Grief and Loss in the Workplace

Grief in the workplace is a topic that is often forgotten but that is very real and can cause a great deal of pain and frustration for the bereaved. Some employers are very sympathetic to their employees when a death occurs in their families or when a death occurs in the workplace and their coworkers are affected; others may do very little to help their employees. Typically, when a death occurs in an employee's family or to an employee in the workplace, the bereaved usually get a few days off from work and then are expected to go back to their lives and function the best they can.

The problem is, it's really hard to function at all, let alone at the level of expectation placed by others. The "fog of death"—the numb, shocked, how-did-this-happen state immediately following a death—can last for days or weeks or even months. Unfortunately, even though the bereaved are not able to really function at work, fears of losing their jobs can become very real.

This predicament, whether it is because of a death in a family or a coworker's death, is what many bereaved face when they return to work and try to concentrate and function normally. What can employers do to help employees who are grieving? Having a bereavement policy in place and providing workers access to counseling or grief support services would benefit not only the affected workers, but also their coworkers, management teams, and the workplace environment overall.

Employees, as well as their employers, benefit when their employers are considerate enough to offer help in coping with grief and loss issues in the workplace. Employers who do not offer to help their employees while they are grieving could be harming morale, hindering employee job satisfaction, and eventually causing a problem with productivity in the workplace.

Everything might look normal on the surface, but after looking deeper, we find the employer may be paying a large price for not addressing grief issues in the workplace.

What kinds of problems might this cause? Employers could lose valuable, skilled, experienced employees who quit after a less-than-compassionate experience during a time of grief. The environment in the workplace can take on a cold, insensitive feeling that lacks compassion and understanding, making other employees feel self-conscious and awkward. Grieving employees might experience more intense emotional and even physical health problems than what they might have had if the employer had been more compassionate. Finally, overall productivity could go down as employees become more disconnected because of the underlying grief and the range of emotions that could arise.

Estimated costs for ignoring grief and related factors can add up to billions of dollars annually because of such causes as missing work due to depression after a death, reduced productivity, absenteeism, and an increase in job stress.

After a loss, an employee's perception of their employer can make a big difference in the employee's job satisfaction and whether or not the individual will stay in their position or look for another. Employees who don't feel appreciated or cared about tend to have a diminished work ethic and are more likely to look for another job instead of trying to make things work.

As terrible as it may sound, some employers are willing to talk about grief issues with their employees because they know that it could profit productivity and could create more benefits for the company. The loss of an employee, especially due to a personal issue such as grief, can have a definite ripple effect within the workplace. When one person suffers a loss, it often affects more than just one employee in the workplace; in fact, it is possible for the entire work environment to be affected.

Employers would be wise to provide compassion, flexibility, and resources to their workers after a death. Whether a business is a large corporation with a human resources department that can provide specific assistance and resources for the bereaved or a small company in which the owner or senior leadership needs to step up, a positive environment for grieving employees should include the following:

- Established, proactive steps and protocols about bereavement and the discussion of grief issues.
- A compassionate format for remembering, discussing, and honoring deceased colleagues.
- A compassionate person who will reach out to the bereaved individual(s) about logistics, meals, or other immediate tasks that need to be completed either in the personal or professional setting.
- Counseling resources that can be provided or covered by the employer.
- A designated person or group of people who will provide training for leaders, managers, and coworkers about the proper things to say and not to say after a death.

No employer is immune to loss, and no one can anticipate when a loss will occur. It can happen to anyone at any time, which is why it is so important to have a plan already in place. Often, an employee just needs someone to listen to them or, in the case of a deceased employee, some way to acknowledge and honor the deceased coworker in the workplace. When employers begin to take on an active role in assisting their employees with the grieving process, everyone benefits. When employers bring stability back to the workplace and show their concern to their employees, the employees begin to feel valued again, and often, things begin to flow somewhat smoother again.

Death of an Employee

When an employee dies, it can be very difficult for everyone in that particular workplace. Many people become very close to their coworkers and often share stories about their backgrounds, interests, and personal lives. But when a death occurs in the workplace, the daily routine changes: instead of being greeted by a coworker, employees might instead be greeted by silence because their friend and colleague is no longer there to welcome them, share stories, ask for advice, or help them with their work. Employees who shared workspaces with the deceased can become distracted by their emotions that can run from to dismay to devastation.

The death of an employee also has productivity repercussions related to their specific jobs and tasks. Their work might need to be deciphered, divided, and distributed to other workers who must pick up where the deceased employee left off. The empty desk of a deceased associate can be a painful and difficult reminder for the entire team. The workplace may need to be changed around to enable these colleagues to work again.

The main objective is to lessen the impact on those left behind by eliminating the presence of an empty chair without having to sacrifice the dignity and reverence for the person who has died. In addition to changing the environment, the abandoned cubicle or desk needs to be cleaned out and reassigned to someone else. This could be awkward and devastating to the person who now has to sit in that spot when they know everyone will be looking at them and wishing their colleague was still sitting there instead. It is very important for a supervisor or manager to make time for people to get together, share memories and feelings, and, in some way, honor their deceased coworker. This could occur on breaks or on longer lunch hours. They need to be able to talk, remember, and share their feelings without fear of repercussions related to productivity and "the job."

What are some strategies for helping manage grief in the workplace when an employee has died? Here are some suggestions:

- Communication is key. Let employees know as soon as possible that one of their coworkers has died.
- Encourage calls or visits to the family of the person who died—as individuals or in small groups, perhaps two or three at a time.
- Provide release time, allowing employees to attend the funeral or memorial services.
- Designate a private place in the office for employees to grieve during the workday.
- Be aware of different ethnic, cultural, and religious bereavement practices represented by those in the workplace.
- Suggest that the team or a group of coworkers work together to clean out a coworker's desk (or be available to help a family member do it).
- Relax productivity requirements or goals for a period of time, allowing the team to adjust to the loss of their coworker.

Death of an Employee's Family Member

Whether it is an employee or an employee's family member who dies, there should already be a policy in place that any employee who wishes to take off work for the funeral will not be penalized in any way, such as having their pay docked or having to use their vacation or sick leave. This could also be applied to bosses or managers. After the funeral is over, the bereaved should be allowed to take their time coming back to work; if they are pressured to return too soon, whether it's the next day or the next week, they will likely not be able to perform up to their normal standards or to management's standards. If possible, they should be allowed to have flexible hours when they do return and the freedom to attend a grief support group or, if necessary, an employee assistance program during work hours.

A high degree of sensitivity and compassion from employers and coworkers is crucial for an employee who is grieving. The bereaved could return to work feeling distracted, anxious, angry, depressed, and unable to concentrate. These are normal signs of grief, but if management and coworkers don't realize that, then the bereaved could be in for some difficult times at work. Grief reactions can be very unpredictable, and the bereaved may feel embarrassed or have to leave when they begin to cry and can't seem to stop. More importantly, each situation must be handled individually, because not everyone grieves the same way. Although it's important to have policies in place, it's even more important to have compassion and flexibility that will benefit each unique situation when an employee suffers a loss.

Everyone handles grief differently. Some bereaved might want to talk about the deceased, while others may not be able to discuss the deceased at all because it is too painful for them at work. If there is no trust or sense of compassion between management and fellow coworkers, the bereaved may not feel free to talk about how they are truly feeling for fear of what may happen to them. They do not want to be the "topic around the water cooler." They do, however, want to grieve and not be forced to share their feelings if they are not ready or don't feel safe doing so. Neither do they want to be avoided, shunned, or told how they should feel, or hear others compare their losses to theirs and rush them to "get over it and move on."

It would be a good idea to have a grief counselor or someone from employee assistance set up an in-service program about what to do when a death occurs so that there will already be a plan in place, giving everyone in the company a better idea of what to do and what to expect when a death does occur. This in-service program could, in addition to other topics, explain how to talk to and listen to the bereaved as well as share the importance of not giving them advice and not using euphemisms, metaphors, or clichés when talking with the them because it could be very offensive to the bereaved as well as to their families. Because life and death occurs in all facets of our lives, we will come across coworkers, friends, and acquaintances who are grieving. Although society recognizes the impact of the death of a spouse, child, or family member, death outside of the immediate family is not always acknowledged. We need to acknowledge and recognize the pain caused by the death of not only parents, siblings, and family members, but also of mentors, business partners, best friends, and fellow workers, as well as many other types of relationships in the workplace.

Death in the Workplace

When death in a workplace occurs onsite, especially a violent death, such as a shooting or a bombing, the perceived safety of the workplace is damaged for workers. Employees may witness rescue and recovery efforts or crime scene investigations. These destructive and discordant activities in the workplace add to the devastation, confusion, and anxiety employees are already feeling; additionally, they may be suffering from sleep disturbances, cognitive impairments, and a sudden change in their world views or core assumptions about how life should be.

As workers approach their workplaces, they could be grieving the losses of their coworkers, friends, and possibly even family members, which could cause anything to trigger a painful reaction for them. Short-term crisis interventions, such as in-service trauma groups, on-site counselors, and employee assistance personnel to listen to their pain and try to reassure them that they will get through these tragedies together, could improve their healing and help them to return to work sooner, thereby minimizing the negative impact of increased absenteeism and low productivity.

Workers could also be helped with their healing and recovery if mental health providers and other organizations would collaborate with each other effectively when they provide services and resources to public tragedies or any trauma or loss that occurs.

Survivors face a possible increased risk of pathological grief, such as shock or an inability to function or understand what is going on around them—especially when their grief was caused by sudden, violent, or traumatic events. Normalizing these reactions and educating workers about the grief process, providing coping strategies, and emphasizing the importance of building and strengthening their social support networks would be very beneficial for them as they process their grief.

Small groups are very effective in handling the needs of workers going through significant emotional distress after a tragedy occurs. These ongoing groups are capable of stabilizing individuals in acute crises by allowing participants to vent their feelings, increasing social support, and teaching coping skills. Small group support in the workplace can also be helpful, especially if the group meets over a lunch hour or immediately after work, which would make it easier to attend.

Large or small groups can also be a way for employees to learn how to anticipate incidents that may cause a setback in their healing. For example, triggers, such as anniversary dates, specific scenarios, interactions with the same client as when the death occurred, or other circumstances are likely, and having a reaction to them is normal, even if the bereaved doesn't put the connection together immediately. Many of the bereaved have no idea as to why they feel the way they do; group sessions or individualized grief counseling could help them to form a plan and be prepared as to how they might be able to handle different situations that are triggers for them.

The sooner employers reach out to the bereaved and get them the help they need, the sooner they will heal and productivity in the workplace will once again continue to thrive.

Chapter References

Everly, G.S. Jr., G. S., Latin, J. M., & Mitchell, J. T. (2000). Innovations in group crisis intervention. In A. R. Roberts (Ed.), *Crisis intervention handbook: Assessment, treatment and research* (2nd ed.). New York: Oxford University Press.

Foy, D. W., Glynn, S. M., Schnurr, P. P., Jankowski, M. K., Wattenberg, M. S., Weiss, D. S., Marmar, C. R., & Gusman, F. D. (2000). In E. B. Foa, T. M. & M.J. Freidman (Eds.), *Effective treatments for PTSD* (pp. xxx–xxx). New York: Guilford Press.

*Hofsees, R. (2002). Grief and loss in the workplace. *The Forum: Association of Death Education and Counseling.*

*Kodanz, R. (2000). *Grief in the workplace* Colorado Springs, CO: Bereavement Publishing.

Rando, T. A. (1996). In K. J. Doka (Ed.), *Living with grief after sudden loss: Suicide, homicide, accident, heart attack, and stroke.* Washington, D.C.: Hospice Foundation of America.

Stein, E., & Eisen, B. (1996). Helping trauma survivors cope: Effects of immediate brief co-therapy and crisis intervention. *Crisis Intervention, 3*, 113–127.

Williams, M. B., & Nurmi, L. A. (1997). Death of a co-worker: Facilitating the healing. In C. R. Figley, B. E., & N. Mazza (Eds.), *Death and Trauma: The traumatology of grieving.* Bristol, PA: Taylor & Francis.

*Zucker, R. (2009). Grieving the death of a co-worker. *Care notes.* St. Meinrad, IN: Abbey Press.

* See Annotated References for a short description of this resource.

CHAPTER 9

The Language of Bereavement

We live in a death-denying society that uses language and terminology that could be very detrimental and have a great impact on those who are grieving. The negativity surrounding this type of language is often what the bereaved remember and carry with them as they try to cope. It is difficult to cope with a loss when you hear, read, or encounter the language of bereavement that they are faced with from some family members, friends, or professionals, as well as different types of media. Language is very powerful and can make a difference in how we see the world depending on whether it is positive or negative; therefore, it is important to use positive language when speaking to the bereaved to help them as they try to cope with the deaths of their loved ones. It is important to remember that grief takes as long as it takes and that everyone grieves differently; in other words, what works for one person does not necessarily work for another.

The word *bereavement* comes from the root word *reave*, which means "to tear up" or "to rend." It is as if something very important to us has been suddenly ripped away by a disruptive force. It feels like a part of ourselves has been stripped away from us against our will—like being robbed.

As the bereaved experience this terrible feeling, their responses to their losses are called grief. Their emotions, thoughts, and feelings result in physical, behavioral, mental, and spiritual responses. Grief is a process during which the bereaved come to terms with the deaths of their loved ones as well as contemplate what their lives will be moving forward. It is not an easy time; neither is it a prescribed length, which is what can cause the support of friends and family to wane. The support and care extended immediately after a death begins to wane as those not as affected by the death move on with their lives in a timely fashion (in their own minds). But for the bereaved, the timing doesn't mean anything. They still struggle through each day, facing their new realities, trying to figure out what's next in life. The bereaved may feel (either consciously or subconsciously) that others are rushing them through their grief because they feel uncomfortable with the grieving process. These "supporters" may tell those who are bereaved what to do and how to feel to "get over it." Is it any wonder that the bereaved feel no one is truly listening to them after someone has died? When they finally decide to go public and share their ongoing grief, they are often made to feel that they should keep their feelings to themselves because they are making so many people sad or unhappy by the way they are acting. It is not surprising that they do not publicly share their true feelings because of the fear, embarrassment, and anxiety they encounter.

The dying and the bereaved are all around us. If we would simply take a few minutes to stop, listen, and look around, we would see so many people who are hurting and who are trying hard to cope, in spite of many of the obstacles they face. Sometimes, no matter where they seem to turn, they are surrounded with reminders and opinions of how they should feel or act. A good example of this is in the media. One simply has to look at the negative way death is treated by the news or entertainment media on television and in movies to see how superficial the topic of death has become in our society.

The journalistic stance, "If it bleeds, it leads," usually sets the stage for media coverage of horrific deaths that lead to revictimization or a second trauma after the first trauma actually happens. Reporters try to capture the experience of a trauma from as many viewpoints as possible, often at the expense of the victims or survivors. How many times have you heard these insensitive questions posed by the media to a survivor of a tragic accident? Comments like "How do you feel seeing your husband and child crushed behind the wheel?" or "What will you do now that your husband and child were not able to get out alive?" highlight the lack of respect and empathy for the bereaved's loss and unexpected reality. How does a person who is in shock and mental, emotional, and possibly physical pain respond to a senseless question? Does what she or he feels really matter, or is this yet another sensational story for the media? The depersonalization of the tragedy by treating it as "just another news item" makes the actual reality for those affected even harsher and more uncompassionate. It seems that the more we become desensitizated to the tragic deaths around us, the more we seem to lack true compassion for the bereaved.

Sometimes, even the language that people use when talking about death and dying seems to be in the form of a euphemism. The words *died* and *dying* are often avoided because when they are mentioned, it sounds permanent and difficult to say, whereas when other phrases are used, such as the euphemism "passed away," it doesn't seem real and waters down the idea that death is final. Other examples include such phrases as "the deceased has been laid to rest"; burial becomes "an interment"; the body becomes "the remains"; and terminal care has become "palliative care" (a term that is often confusing to people).

Even sympathy cards are a way for people to express their sympathies to the bereaved without having to directly mention death. Some cards refer to death metaphorically, such as "What is death but a long sleep?" Another card might say, "He is not dead; he is just away." The first phrase suggests a long sleep, suggesting that perhaps the person will awaken at some point. The second phase refers to simply being away, perhaps on a trip, but that the person could possibly return. Neither is correct.

The use of language can also enlighten us about the intensity and immediacy of what a person encounters with death through their stories about brushes with death. A person's word choice can reflect changes in how a death event happened and is experienced at different times. In fact, language often gives clues about the manner of death and the speaker's attitude toward the death.

Even children deal with cartoon depictions of death such as the "classic" Wile E. Coyote, Daffy Duck, Bugs Bunny, and Elmer Fudd. All these characters and many others show children how death seems to be reversible. Wile E. Coyote, for example, gets smashed to pieces and always comes back to life. Daffy Duck is pressed into a thin sheet by a steamroller; Elmer Fudd aims and shoots Bugs Bunny, and Bugs Bunny is hit but jumps up as good as new—reversing death. How can young children believe in the finality of death when what they see on television is that the dead don't die? Is it any wonder that when a real death happens in their lives, they are confused as to why the deceased person did not come back like their cartoon friends did?

Westerns also depict something on a fantasy level and use clichés surrounding death, such as when the bad guys are killed in a gun battle and they describe this as "kicking the bucket"; and Boot Hill is where the bad guys are buried or are said to be "pushing up daisies." Then there are the horror films, known as "death porn," which have become a very profitable form of moviemaking with films such as *Dead Teenager, Slasher, Nightmare on Elm Street, Psycho,* and *Silence of the Lambs.*

It seems that no matter where we go in the world, what we do, or what we watch on TV or read in the media, we cannot escape death and the different ways it is portrayed. Social scientists believe we are lagging behind in meeting new challenges resulting in social change. However, today's globalization gives us much information from a great distance about those who have died far away from the comfort of our own homes. We seem to be confronted with death whether we want to know about it or not. Even though our attitudes toward death grow and develop through life, it has been said that, "The most precious thing in life is its uncertainty," which is what the bereaved deal with every day of their lives. This uncertainty is not the loss of their loved ones, but rather, about who they are now that their loved ones have died and what meaning life holds for them now and in the future.

What can the bereaved do to help with some of this uncertainty and negative language that they seem to face daily? Here are some suggestions:

- Be around positive people, those you trust who will listen and not tell you how you should feel.
- No one can grieve 24/7, so step back and do something you enjoy or would like to try, such as painting, gardening, fishing, golf, or other hobbies or activities.
- Do something for someone else.
- Call a friend and go for a walk or a run.
- Take your dog for a walk.
- Eat at least two healthy meals each day to give you strength to get through the day.
- Find a quiet place to rest or mediate.

If you think you need to talk to someone professionally, make an appointment with a grief therapist or grief counselor. It may be helpful to have someone listen with an objective ear and to know that you have been heard.

Laugh whenever you get the chance, and do not apologize for how you feel. You have a right to feel what you feel, including laughing or crying when you need to.

Chapter References

Harvey, A. D. (1986). Evidence of a tense shift in personal experiences narratives. *Empirical Studies of the Arts, 4*(2), 151–162.

DeSpelder, L. A., & Strickland A. L. (2014). *The last dance: Encountering death and dying.* Mountain View; CA: Mayfield.

Fulton, R., & Owen, G. (1987). Death & society in twentieth century America. *Omega: Journal of Death & Dying, 18(4).*

Keen, S. (1986). *Faces of the enemy: Reflections of the hostile imagination.* San Francisco: Harper & Row.

*Tate, F. B. (1989). Impoverishment of death symbolism: The negative consequences. *Death Studies, 13*(3), 305–306.

* See Annotated References for a short description of this resource.

CHAPTER 10

Triggers—Anniversaries, Birthdays, Holidays

What are triggers? Triggers, or "grief spasms," as they are often called, occur when everything seems to be going along okay and the bereaved are finally beginning to feel they have a handle on their grief. It is at that point when the anniversary of a marriage, death, or even when the diagnosis occurred that the bereaved seem to take one step forward and three steps back. It may feels as though they have just been punched in the stomach and that their grief is starting all over again.

Birthdays and holidays seem to have the same effect on the bereaved as anniversaries and other special days because, for the bereaved, it really makes no difference; it is still difficult. However, anniversaries, birthdays, and holidays are not the only triggers for the bereaved: a phone call from a business or telemarketer who wants to speak to the deceased may require the bereaved to explain that the person whom they seek has died. Or a magazine may continue to be mailed with the deceased's name on the cover despite that the bereaved spouse has already tried, unsuccessfully, to cancel the subscription. When the bereaved walk down the street, through a store, or through the mall and see someone wearing the same kind of outfit that their loved ones once wore, the bereaved might think it could be their loved ones, still alive. Or when the bereaved are at church or are driving or walking and see a couple holding hands and realize that this is no longer possible for them with their loved ones. Or perhaps they turn on the radio and it plays a song that their loved ones enjoyed singing or dancing to. These triggers can go on and on for the bereaved and cause a setback in their grief if they are not careful.

The anticipation of birthdays, anniversaries, or the holidays are often more troublesome than the actual death. However, the long commercial buildup to the holidays—the constant reminders, such as holiday decorations in all the stores, greeting cards on the shelves, holiday displays and discounts on toys and other gifts, holiday movies, Christmas tree sales on every other street corner, and discussion about gifts and parties, can cause considerable stress and sadness. In other words, it seems that no matter where they go or what they do, they can't hide from the holidays.

Several strategies can help the bereaved during the holidays, as well as with the anticipation of birthdays and anniversaries. It is a matter of taking control of the situation and being prepared:

- The most important thing to do is have a *plan*. In fact, have plans A, B, and even C, if necessary—anything that will help the day go smoother. If one plan doesn't work, it is always good to have another one standing by; this helps with some anxiety that can occur during the holidays; even doing nothing and staying home can be a plan.
- Talk with family and friends before the scheduled events to let them know how difficult this might be for you and that you might have to leave early. It is a good idea to drive yourself to these events, if possible, so that if you do have to leave early your host or hostess is aware and no one feels obligated to leave the event to take you home.
- You are not obligated to go to every party or even to any party; you decide.

- If everyone always comes to your house for dinner, suggest meeting at someone else's house for a potluck, going out to dinner, or, if you are usually always the cook, invite others to bring their favorite dishes for the meal instead of cooking everything yourself. Perhaps, rather than going to someone's house for dinner, you could go over for dessert or have the host or hostess come over to your house after everyone leaves.
- If you have always sent Christmas cards, decorated the house, or done a lot of baking, this might be the year for a change. You could opt not to send cards or not as many. You don't have to decorate as much—or at all, if you don't want to. Instead of baking, you could go out and buy a pie or dessert. Remember, you can always change back next year.
- Take care of yourself and don't put expectations on yourself that will cause you additional stress.
- Do something to honor your loved one's memory, such as giving money in their name to a charity they liked or to your loved one's place of worship; have a Mass said for them; light a candle in your loved one's memory; go to dinner and raise a glass in their memory; have a scholarship set up in the deceased's name at their high school, college, or trade school; or donate books in their memory to a library.
- Try very hard to keep only positive people around you, especially during the holidays and other special events in your life—those people who will allow you to cry or feel what you feel without telling you to move on or to get over your loved one's death.
- If you had been to a support group before, it might be a good idea to go again during the holidays for some extra support.

The holidays can be especially difficult, as they are traditionally times when families gather in anticipation of enjoying time together. The holidays are supposed to be happy, loving, and full of fun; and they are generally times of positive emotions (or are expected to be). But those who have suffered the loss of a loved one may struggle to feel these happy emotions. Family or friends could help the bereaved to prepare themselves for several holiday-related dilemmas that may trigger their grief and give them permission not to feel guilty for feeling sad:

Being Happy and Cheerful. There seems to be an expectation that everyone should be happy and cheerful during the holidays. The bereaved need to allow themselves to feel what they feel, whether it's happy, sad, cheerful, unhappy, or any other emotion, without having to feel they must meet the expectations of others. The bereaved should never have to apologize or explain how they feel; they have a right to their emotions.

The Minefield of Social Exchange. The innocent comments of others, especially of someone who is not aware that an individual has experienced a loss, could cause a great deal of pain to the bereaved because others feel this is a time for everyone to be happy. The bereaved can be thrown off guard by the comments of complete strangers, such as, "Hope you and your family have a wonderful holiday." This sounds like a wonderful greeting, but when someone has died, this greeting is very difficult to hear. The bereaved need to be prepared for what might be said to them when they go to someone's house over the holidays, especially with the possibility that strangers might not be aware of their losses. If they are prepared, they can respond in a way that makes them feel comfortable doing so.

The Complexity of Decisions. The bereaved must decide what to do and what not to do when it comes to dealing with decisions about family activities and rituals. For example, a simple gesture, such as whether or not to hang the Christmas stocking of a young child who died, sending holiday cards to family and friends, or even whether to decorate a tree, may cause problems for the bereaved. Remember, there is no right or wrong answer; the bereaved need to do what makes them feel comfortable, not what everyone else thinks they should do or not do. For instance, if they have always sent out holiday cards but they just don't have the energy this year, then perhaps this is the year not to send cards out. This holiday ritual can always be resumed the following year.

Decorating a tree can bring back many memories of family gatherings and the deceased; perhaps this year, the bereaved could decorate a very small tree (one that sits on a table with specific ornaments in memory of the deceased) or have no tree at all. Remember, this is a decision that must be made by the bereaved, and there is no right or wrong answer. It is entirely up to the bereaved and what they feel comfortable with.

The Ambush. These are events that are unexpected and unpredictable. They are often called grief attacks or zingers. Something as simple as coming across an ornament with a child's handprint, hearing a much-loved song, or finding a photo of the deceased from the Christmas prior to their death can be overwhelming to someone who is grieving. The grief can become fresh again and can take over completely. It would help the bereaved to know these ambushes are not only possibilities, but are likely to happen. Often, having someone to help the bereaved with their decorating provides support and a shoulder to cry on that they may need at that time.

Successfully navigating through the holidays, no matter how many years have gone by, can be done by having a plan (or two or three), taking control, making their wishes known to their family and friends early, as well as being aware of the potential for ambush events.

Triggers can happen no matter where the bereaved are in their grief process. However, over time, trigger events—whether birthdays, anniversaries, holidays, or even parts of one's normal daily life, often become less difficult, and the bereaved are able to be more in control, experience less pain, and celebrate life once again.

Chapter References

Noel, B., & Blair, P. D. (2000). *I wasn't ready to say goodbye.* Vancouver, WA: Champion Press.

*Wortman, C. (2009). Getting through the holiday: Advice for the bereaved. *University of Phoenix: WGBH Educational Foundation and Vulcan Productions, Inc.* https://www.utmb.edu/caps/grief-loss/getting-through-the-hoildays.

* See Annotated References for a short description of this resource.

CHAPTER 11

Disenfranchised Grief and Ambiguous Loss

Ethel's dog dies. Her adult daughter wonders if her constant tears and other displays of grief are evidence of senility.

Rory is a young man with substantial developmental disabilities. His siblings discuss whether or not to share the information with him that his father has died. There is no discussion, however, about the fact that they all believe he should not attend the funeral.

Neighbors are uncertain about how to respond to the impending death of the Anders' son. Normally, they would send a flower arrangement and collect money for the family. But the Anders' son is sentenced to be executed on Thursday. They are torn about how to acknowledge the situation and about whether they should do anything at all.

Tom's longstanding lover, Paul, dies. Paul's family arranges the funeral. Though Tom is acknowledged as a "friend," he has little role in the funeral. He has to take vacation days from work in order to attend.

Ethel, Rory, the Anders family, and Tom have all experienced a loss, but because of a variety of misapplied reasoning, their losses are not recognized by others as losses worthy of grieving. This is what it means to have a *disenfranchised loss*. These and other similar instances create great pain because the survivors are not allowed or do not have the right to grieve because society does not sanction or support their losses.

Disenfranchised losses typically fit into one of four broad categories: **The relationship is not recognized.** Relationships such as lovers, friends, neighbors, foster parents, colleagues, in-laws, step-parents and step-children, caregivers, counselors, siblings, roommates, and residents of a nursing home all fall into this category. Basically, society in general and employers do not allow for time to grieve these losses.

The loss is not acknowledged. These losses refer to situations such as perinatal death, miscarriage, spontaneous abortion, placing children in adoption or foster care, the death of a pet, or grief experienced from later stages of ALS (Amyotrophic Lateral Sclerosis) or other diseases. Some losses do not include death, such as the loss of a body part, the loss of a job, infertility, empty nest syndrome, or divorce. These losses have grief attached to them as well, but they often go unrecognized or ignored.

When a miscarriage or infant death occurs, the entire family suffers. Every day, millions of women experience miscarriages, and no one knows. Many in the medical field think of a miscarriage as just a "small sack of cells." What a terrible way to tell a parent that their child-to-be has died. These bereaved parents experience grief like everyone else, often for a lifetime. This is a loss society doesn't recognize as "grief-worthy," and we certainly don't offer the parents much comfort in their sadness. In many cases, men are not even recognized as having experienced a loss, only women. How sad to have to experience society's stigma and lack of compassion. This child-to-be was conceived like any other, with love and anticipation of the future, only to die in utero, often with no warning or reason.

Women who have either experienced a miscarriage or know others who have may be afraid to tell anyone they are expecting for fear that something terrible might happen and their child will die, and no one will understand, or they will simply be ignored. Other moms are more willing to share about their losses because they understand the unique bond between a mother and baby and that no one can really understand the pain except another mom suffering from a perinatal loss.

Additionally, grandparents who suffer the death of a grandchild are thought of as "forgotten grievers." What many do not realize or consider is that grandparents grieve twice: once for their adult child who is grieving, and once for their child's child (i.e., their grandchild) who died—yet, not much attention is given to the grief of the grandparents.

The griever is excluded. In these situations, the person is thought to be incapable of grief, or others assume that the griever wouldn't understand the circumstances. These include the very old, the very young, and those with developmental disabilities or mental illnesses. Not only are they excluded from the grieving process, but they may not be told anything about why the deceased is no longer a part of their lives, creating additional confusion.

The circumstances of the death. These would include instances of suicide, AIDS, execution, homicide, the death of an alcoholic, death by overdose, and SIDS (Sudden Infant Death Syndrome). These deaths tend to carry a negative connotation and are not typically supported or accepted by society.

In all or most of these situations, there is no recognized role in which the bereaved can assert the right to grieve and to mourn, and therefore, they receive no social support. A stigma is attached to many of these types of deaths, and survivors are shunned rather than accepted. In some cases, the mourner may not be allowed to attend the funeral or have any part in planning the ritual.

In bereavement and grief, those who are disenfranchised are denied the legitimacy and freedoms that come with social approval and sanction. Thoughtless comments such as, "Don't feel that way"; "Try not to think those thoughts"; or "You shouldn't act that way" are common in a disenfranchised loss. Society often strongly suggests that the bereaved should keep their grief reactions private so as not to upset those around them—especially when the deaths they are grieving (according to society) don't appear to qualify for grief in the first place.

Coping strategies such as continuing to mourn, memorializing, ritualizing, and doing whatever the bereaved can to find peace, comfort, and resolution in their losses, whether society recognizes these losses or not, can be very difficult for the bereaved. Those who grieve disenfranchised losses are often misunderstood for how they act; therefore, society does not value or acknowledge them. Some bereaved individuals have been told not to continually go over the details of an accident and that they need to forget what happened and move on. This presumes that someone can simply move on without being affected by the death.

If we enhance our understanding of disenfranchisement in bereavement and grief, we might then be able to contribute to improving an appreciation of this concept's potential breadth and depth. Listening and understanding teaches us to be more sensitive and to remember that we should not devalue important aspects of the bereaveds' experiences. Grief is, after all, the expression of valuing what we have lost.

Ambiguous Loss

Ambiguous loss is similar to disenfranchised loss in that there is uncertainty surrounding the loss. The difference is that with an ambiguous loss, the question is not about whether the bereaved has the right to grieve, but whether a loss has occurred in the first place. Uncertainty makes ambiguous loss the most anxious of all losses, causing symptoms that are painful but most often missed or misdiagnosed. **There are two types of Ambiguous loss. This type of ambiguous loss occurs when loved ones are physically absent but psychologically present: there is no proof of death, but neither is the person physically present.** Examples include situations when planes or helicopters are missing or have crashed, when soldiers are missing in action or children are kidnapped, when children are separated from their families, when there is a tragic train or car accident, or even a severe storm and families and friends do not know if their loved ones are dead or alive. It's the not knowing that causes a great deal of distress.

Another type of ambiguous loss occurs when the person is physically present but psychologically absent, examples such as someone in a coma, in late stages of Alzheimer's or other progressive diseases, in addiction, or suffering from AIDS, a stroke, a brain injury, or a chronic mental illness. It could also be the result of a person who does not recognize anyone from before an accident because they experienced serious head trauma that resulted in short- or long-term memory loss.

Reactions to ambiguous loss are complicated, simply because the situation is not clearly defined. Uncertainty is coupled with hope and can alternate between despair and fervent belief in a positive outcome. Emotional outbursts and complete withdrawal are normal. Frantic activity, such as searching for a missing person, contacting those who could help with the search, and getting the word out to as many people as possible can be followed by even more frustration. Uncertainty can get in the way of coping mechanisms.

The bereaved cannot start grieving because the situation is not yet determined. The confusion paralyzes the grieving process. People go from hope to hopelessness and back again. It is like they are frozen in time and can't move one way or the other. Depression and anxiety often take over. These symptoms can affect one person or the whole family.

In cases of ambiguous loss, closure is important. The families are in limbo and need to see an end to their fears, anger, confusion, and frustration. This can come only through some kind of resolution, intervention, or closure of their loved ones' situations, such as getting some word about where they are, how they are, or that they have died. In most cases, not knowing is worse than knowing, even if death is the tragic truth. Bringing clarity to an ambiguous loss situation is the only way a family can either move on to help their loved ones recover or begin grieving their deaths. Until they know one way or the other, they are stuck in between, which is a very difficult place to be.

Everyone deals with their grief in different ways, and ambiguous loss is no different. Not having any information one way or the other makes situations impossible to actually know how to feel or what to do—except perhaps to pray, not to give up hope, and continue to inquire about the missing loved ones, whether it is through local, state, or national resources.

It is also important to continue talking within the family and to come up with solutions that might bring peace to everyone involved, such as using the internet to find information; lobbying congressmen to make changes in laws, such as with immigration or missing children; hiring a detective to get more information; or talking with others experiencing the same loss in case they have information or a new clue. Seeking answers often helps to ease the stress and anxiety of not knowing. It is important to do whatever you think you must do to find peace and know in your heart that you have done everything you could to get answers. When your heart and mind come together and you feel you have done everything possible to resolve the situation, then perhaps it is time to move on for the time being. The most important thing is to avoid feeling hopeless as well as helpless in your ambiguous loss.

Chapter References

*Boss, P. (1999). *Ambiguous loss*. Cambridge, MA: Harvard University Press.

Corr, C. A. (1998). Enhancing the concept of disenfranchised grief. *Omega, 38, 1–20.*

Doka, K. J. (2002). *Living with grief: Loss in later life.* Washington, D.C.: Hospice Foundation of America.

Doka, K. J. (1989). *Disenfranchised grief: Recognizing hidden sorrows.* Lexington, MA: Lexington Books.

Doka, K. J. (2002). Disenfranchised Grief (New Directions, Challenges, and Strategies for Practice). Champaign, Illinois: Research Press

*Folta, C., & Deck, D. (1976). Grief, the funeral and the friend. In V. Pine, A. H. Kutsscher, and R. C. Peretz, (Eds.), *Acute grief and the funeral,* Springfield, IL: Charles C. Thomas.

Parkes, C. M. (2001). *Bereavement: Studies of grief in adult life* (3rd ed.). New York: Routledge

*Rando, T.A. (1993). *The treatment of complicated mourning.* Champaign, IL: Research Press.

* See Annotated References for a short description of this resource.

CHAPTER 12

Funeral Etiquette and Religious Customs

Individuals and families often experience a great deal of sadness and emotional pain when their loved ones die. They go through periods of numbness and denial right after the death and for weeks and possibly months to follow. At first, they may have a hard time remembering who was at the visitation or prayer service or even the funeral. Many times, they even struggle with what is said to them; however, they do seem to remember the negative comments people say to them. Unfortunately, many individuals do not know what to say or how to act around the bereaved at a visitation or a funeral—or even in the weeks and months after the funeral—and can cause many negative feelings that can last for a long time, possibly even ending a relationship.

What is proper funeral etiquette? Funeral etiquette is basically what to do and not to do at a visitation or a funeral. There are many things that could occur at these services that could be offensive to a family member you are greeting in the visitation line or at the funeral, such as, if you should decide to give the bereaved a hug, first be sure the person is okay with hugging. There are some people who don't want to hug and who would rather just shake your hand instead. Hugging can be very offensive to others and make them feel uncomfortable and unsure of what to do next, especially if they are not the "hugging type." Ideally, it would be best to ask them if it is okay to give them a hug and then you will know how to respond.

Another thing that could cause the bereaved to feel uncomfortable would be to give them advice, such as how they should feel and what they should do to "get over" this loss. And it is wonderful to chat and tell the family stories of your relationship with the deceased, but remember, you are not the only one in line and you could very well be holding up everyone behind you and making a longer night for the bereaved. Instead, perhaps consider writing a simple note to the family and telling them some stories of you and the deceased. In the long run, this will help the family with their grief. It is okay to cry with family members and express your sympathies as long as you don't get carried away so they end up comforting you rather than you consoling them.

When talking to the bereaved, it is good to say a kind word or two about the deceased. They are struggling enough as it is, so please do *not* use these clichés, euphemisms, or metaphors with them: "You are young enough that you could marry again"; " God needed another flower in his garden, so he took your child"; "He was old or sick and was going to die anyway. He is in a better place now"; "It is a blessing in disguise that your child died now; you don't know what he or she would have been like when he or she grew up."

So, what can you say? "I am sorry for your loss. My sympathies are with you and your family. He/She was a wonderful person and will be greatly missed. I am here for you if you ever want to talk." These are all heartfelt statements that will not cause the bereaved more pain. You should never tell them that you're available to talk if you don't really mean it, because they may take you up on your offer. Sharing a memory or a quality of the deceased that you admired is also a good thing to tell the family. Remember, sympathy is expressed not just through words, but also through actions, such as calling them to check in a few weeks after the funeral, running errands, cleaning, doing yardwork, offering to watch their children, or bringing a meal by their home. One other very helpful but often overlooked way to express sympathy is to simply take time to listen to them.

Children should be allowed to go to the visitation or funeral if they want to go; however, it is the family's responsibility to take care of their children and not let them run around the funeral home or church. Before they go, it will be important to tell the child what they will see and perhaps hear at the funeral home or church so that they will know what to expect upon arrival.

Sign the guest book with your name and address so that the family will know you attended, since they may not remember at the time. They may want to send you a thank you note and may not know your current address.

Sending flowers (or a plant, which lasts longer) is a nice gesture unless the family has stipulated not to, and instead has requested donations in the name of the deceased to their favorite charity. When you send a card, please don't offer advice or suggest how to get over the loss and move on; remember, everyone grieves differently and at their own pace.

What should you wear to a visitation or funeral? In Western society, years ago everyone wore black. Today that is not the case; today, any color is acceptable if it is not too flashy, too bright, or made of glittery fabrics. However, if the deceased was known for a certain type of dress, such as casual wear, jeans, or shirts featuring their favorite sports teams, the family might suggest that everyone dress in that attire. The main thing is to show respect to the family as well as to the deceased.

Religious Customs/Practices

Many religions have different practices and customs surrounding death and burial. For example:

Greek Orthodox: Those in the Greek Orthodox Church believe that death separates the soul from the body and therefore is the start of a new life. The experience enhances the quality of the behavior, character, and communion with God. Most Greek Orthodox funerals involve five parts. First, a wake, held the night before.Next, a funeral service, which takes place at the funeral home with an open casket facing east with the deceased's feet toward the altar. Guests may greet the family, and if you are a believer, you may kiss an icon or a cross that lies on the deceased's breast; those who are nonbelievers are not asked to do so. The burial consists of a brief graveside service with prayers, where each guest places a flower on the casket. Cremation is not allowed. This is followed by a funeral luncheon—referred to as a Makaria, or a mercy meal. Fish is usually served. The next Sunday, the final part occurs, which is a memorial service. The dress is dark and somber for both men and women.

Jewish: An Orthodox Jewish funeral is held at the funeral home or cemetery. Men should cover their heads with yarmulkes (skull caps), and women should cover their heads with scarves. Usually, men and women do not sit together. The Conservative Jewish funeral is at a synagogue; only men must wear yarmulkes; head coverings are optional for women. However, the Reformed Jewish funeral service is in a temple, and it is completely optional to cover one's head. The Orthodox and Conservatives bury their dead the day after the death, whereas the Reformed can wait for a few days.

It is customary for friends and neighbors to prepare the first meal for the bereaved after the funeral and to encourage the bereaved to eat the food prepared for them. If the family uses kosher meal preparation, it is important to follow those food regulations for meals brought to their homes.

Per Jewish custom, flowers are not allowed at a Jewish funeral. If you are planning to visit someone after a death, it should be no later than the Shiva (seven days) period of mourning. These seven days start from the day of the funeral. An hour of the seventh day is considered a full day. Those who visit should see the family within the six days after the funeral. Funerals are not encouraged in the Orthodox synagogues; however, when an Orthodox funeral is held at a funeral home, it is only for a viewing by the immediate family and no one else. At the cemetery, more prayers are read, and then the family members usually participate in placing dirt on the casket before it is buried. This symbolizes their acceptance of the finality of death.

When Orthodox and Conservative families sit Shiva (this is the time when the family sits and receives friends, prays, and talks about the deceased), they are not allowed to leave their homes for any business or social reasons for seven days after the death of their loved ones. They may cover mirrors, burn memorial candles, or wear black ribbons that are cut and that represent the individual breaking away from their loved ones. Men do not shave, and women do not wear makeup. Reformed Jews are not allowed to leave their homes for at least three days after the death of their loved ones. Sitting Shiva represents the disruption that death has brought to their families lives and shows their grief through sacrifice. When Orthodox or Conservative Jewish families leave the cemetery, they wash their hands as a symbol of leaving the dead behind.

Islam: A funeral service for Muslims usually takes place in a mosque. Here, everyone's shoes are removed out of respect. Women and men usually sit separately in designated seats. Women must also wear a head scarf in addition to removing their shoes. Muslims believe in the life hereafter, and death is considered to be Allah's will. They believe that death is not the end, but just a temporary separation of the soul from the body, which will be brought back to life on Judgment Day. When a Muslim hears of someone's death, they say, *"Inna Lillahae wa Inna Elaihae Rajae'uon,"* which means, "Verily, unto Allah do we belong, and verily, unto Him shall we return" (Quran 2:156).

The family and friends gather at the home of the person who has died, give comfort to the family, recite the Quran, and pray for Allah's forgiveness and mercy for the deceased. Muslims believe in burying their dead as soon as possible; cremation and autopsies are forbidden. The body is washed and then prepared for burial. Traditionally in Islam, only the relatives of the deceased may look upon the face of the dead; however, others attending the funeral may not. Friends and family bring the bereaved food and visit with them for the first three days; however, gifts of flowers and candy are not suitable. Non-Muslim friends may show their sympathies and love by being present at the funeral service or by visiting the family. The grieving family would also appreciate hearing the sentiment that Allah shows His mercy to the deceased and forgives them.

Buddhism: Peace and serenity are the distinguishing characteristics of a Buddhist funeral. An altar displays the deceased's picture, along with offerings of candles, incense, flowers, and fruit, as well as an image of the Buddha in front of or beside the altar. A monk usually presides over the rituals. The deceased is usually cremated. During the funeral procession, all attendees should send good thoughts to the family and think about the brevity of life. Black or dark colors are not required at funerals, but it is appropriate to wear conservative clothing; red is frowned upon at funerals. If the funeral takes place in a temple, everyone must remove their shoes out of respect. At the funeral, the family wears white because that is the color of grieving. Anyone planning to attend the funeral service must pay their sympathies to the deceased and the family members before the service at the funeral home.

Hindu: Hindus believe that although the body dies, the individual soul has no beginning and no end. It may pass through reincarnation, depending on one's karma. Hindus would rather die at home, surrounded by their families, who keep vigil. There is an open casket at the funeral, and everyone is expected to see the body. The body usually remains at the home until it is cremated, usually within twenty-four hours after the death. The ashes of the deceased are scattered at a sacred body of water or someplace that is significant to the person who died. The custom at a Hindu funeral is for the family to wear white. However, anyone else who is attending the funeral may wear casual clothing. Flowers are acceptable but not traditional. If the family receives flowers from visitors, they are placed at the feet of the deceased. Friends may visit after the funeral, and the custom is to bring gifts of fruit. The mourning period usually occurs ten to thirty days after the death.

Protestant: For most mainline Protestant faiths, ministry to the bereaved is very important, and flowers are always accepted. Cards or notes of encouragement and stories of the deceased are appreciated. Others are usually welcome to attend the visitation, funeral service (which is usually held at a funeral home or a church), and the committal service at the cemetery—although any of all of these may be private as well; the obituary is the best source of information for this. At the funeral service, there are usually readings and prayers and often a eulogy about the deceased. There is also often a luncheon following the burial at the church that those attending the funeral may be invited to attend. Bringing food to the bereaved's home or sending a donation to a charity or the church in the name of the deceased are other ways to support the family and memorialize the deceased.

Roman Catholic: In the Catholic Church, it is appropriate to attend the wake service and the funeral as well as the burial service (unless it is a private burial). The wake may be held at a funeral home or a church. The visitation or wake can be during the day or evening with the funeral to follow, or the funeral can be the next day at the funeral home or church. Often, there is a luncheon following the burial. Flowers may be sent to the home of the family or the church unless it is specified otherwise. It is also appropriate to have a Mass said for the deceased at a later time, to donate money to their favorite charities, or for the church or light a candle in memory of the the deceased. The funeral is usually a Catholic funeral Mass at the church unless the family specifies that they do not want a Mass; then it will simply be a funeral service at the funeral home. If there is no body present, then it is called a memorial service. Cremation is also allowed in the Catholic Church.

Scientology: There are a number of different funeral ceremonies that could be said over the deceased, or even a sermon or memorial at a service where the body may or may not be present. Scientology sees the spiritual self, which is called the *Thetan*, as being the individual; the body is viewed as a vehicle whereby they interact with each other and the physical universe. The Scientology funeral service is focused on thanking the departed for spending time with us, praising or acknowledging life attributes or achievements, bidding the deceased farewell, and wishing the person well in their future existence. The deceased may be cremated or interred according to the wishes of the family or the deceased. Somber colors can be worn by guests attending the services and casual attire.

Unitarian Universalists: The Unitarian Universalists believe in preplanning funeral and burial arrangements prior to one's death. After this is arranged, it is the responsibility of the individual to talk with their family and put their wishes in writing, where they will be easily found. They can decide on either cremation or body burial; if the person decides to have a body burial, they must request a "green burial" with no embalming chemicals and a simple casket that allows the remains to return to the earth. The individual may also choose to donate their organs or body, but they must make their own arrangements. Most services are held at a church or a funeral home chapel, usually within one week of the death, but they could be up to one month after. Flowers may be sent to the family's home. It is important to sign the guestbook. At the funeral service, leave the first two or three rows of chairs for the deceased's relatives to sit. If you wish to participate in the service, you may; however, it is not necessary. What to wear is decided by the guest attending.

Baha'i: Baha'i funeral services usually take place within two or three days after the death. The Baha'i funeral service consists only of a congregational "Prayer for the Dead." This prayer is read before the burial and is available to the deceased's friends when the "Aqdas" is translated and published. It is vital that the utmost simplicity and flexibility is observed and a selection from the Baha'i sacred writings is read. The Baha'i faith teaches that there is a separate consciousness or soul for every human. Upon death, the soul is relieved of its physical bonds and enters the spiritual world. Those attending these services may wear what they want according to the local custom.

The **Balinese:** For the Balinese, a cremation is an occasion for gaiety and not for mourning because it represents the accomplishment of the most sacred duty, the ceremonial burning of the corpses of the dead to liberate their souls so that they can attain the higher worlds and be free for reincarnation into being better beings. Attire is at the discretion of those attending.

Eastern Orthodox Church in America: In the Orthodox Church in America, a funeral service is usually held three days after the death occurs. Friends can come to the funeral home for one or two days to console the family. Each day before the burial, the priest conducts the "Trisagion Prayers of Mercy" at the wake. After the funeral and the final Trisagion at the cemetery, a Mercy Meal is prepared for the family and friends of the deceased at a restaurant or church. At this time flowers, and donations are made to the Orthodox Church in the name of the person who died. Usually, black or somber clothes are worn to the wake and funeral; however, the priest wears white.

Mormons: Mormons (The Church of Jesus Christ of Latter-day Saints, or LDS) prefer to bury their dead rather than to cremate them. Embalming is allowed, and if the deceased has received their temple endowment, the person can be buried in temple clothes. The funeral takes place in a Latter-day Saints chapel or mortuary by a bishop of the ward. Family members give the family prayer and dedicate the grave but do not have to give a special talk, such as a eulogy. The funeral is said with hope and certainty of what is to come. The funeral is more of a farewell rather than a goodbye, because survivors believe they will see each other again someday.

As you can see, funeral etiquette is very important to the bereaved and to followers of different religions. It is essential for anyone who may attend a funeral different from their own religion to know what to wear, how to act, and what customs await them at the home of the bereaved, and at the funeral home, cemetery, church, mosque, temple, or synagogue.

If you have any questions about any type of funeral etiquette, such as what is appropriate or perhaps expected of you, it would be a good idea to contact the funeral home, the family, or the religious facility where the funeral will take place.

Chapter References

The Funeral Source, (2014). https://www.funeralsource.org.

School of Manners and Common Sense (2006).https://www.a-to-z-of manners-etiquette.com.

Funeral Wise (2005) https://www.funeralwise.com/customs.org.

* See Annotated References for a short description of this resource.

CONCLUSION

In my book, *Comforting the Bereaved Through Listening and Positive Responding*, I have described grief, mourning, and bereavement and have explained how important it is to listen to what the bereaved are trying to tell us as they mourn the loss of their loved ones. I have mentioned ways of coping many different types of death and highlighted the differences among many types of bereaved loved ones. Funeral etiquette and different religious customs pertaining to a death have been discussed as well.

However, even with all this information, I feel that it is of utmost importance to help the bereaved find the path to the right person or group for the help they may need along the way. I suggest seeking out a grief therapist—someone who specializes in the grieving process, not just a therapist who deals with other types of problems such as marriage counseling, behavioral problems, or mental health problems. Often, the bereaved turn to their clergy for help; unfortunately, they may find that many clergy do not have specific training to help them with their grief as they had hoped. A grief therapist will have the training and focus to help the bereaved in ways others may not.

I recommend seeking out an individual grief therapist through a funeral home, hospital, hospice, mental health facility, or even by word of mouth from someone who has been helped through their own grieving experience. The connection and trust between a therapist and the bereaved is vital in order for this relationship to work. It is important for the bereaved to feel that they have been *heard* and not just *listened to*.

Seeking out a grief support group can also be a good idea, but it is important that the bereaved are in the correct group—meaning, all the members share in a similar type of grief. Specific groups include SOS, Survivors of Suicide (family and friends of a loved one who has already ended their lives); SIDS (Sudden Infant Deaths); bereaved parents, parents of murdered children; share pregnancy and infant loss support (death of a baby through pregnancy loss, stillbirth, or in the first few months of life); the death of a pet; grief groups for children, teens, siblings, and older adults; or other special types of grief groups. Some regions have grief support centers where the whole family would have more opportunities to receive help. If you feel your family members would benefit from this, please look for a facility in your area.

Please do not rush the bereaved into seeking help before a month or two has passed since their loss. They need the security and love from family and friends even more in the beginning than they need a professional's help.

I hope this book has been helpful to you and your family and friends. It is my prayer that it has and will continue to bring you peace, comfort, and information that will assist you and the bereaved.

May God Bless you as you comfort the bereaved by listening to them and responding to them in a positive way.

Dr. Dee Stern

APPENDIX A

Mad Bag

The question now becomes, how does someone make one of these mad bags? The materials needed for this project are: a grocery paper bag, newspaper (about two days' worth), red or orange duct tape, heavy string, and a great deal of perseverance. Here are ten simple steps for making a mad bag:

Open the paper bag completely.

Begin crumpling newspaper.

Stuff the crumpled newspaper into the paper bag.

Fill the bag a little over halfway and push the paper down to make it firm.

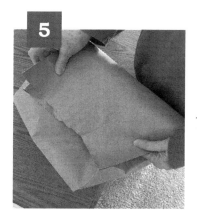

When all of this is completed, then fold the remaining part of the bag over the rest of the bag to form a ball.

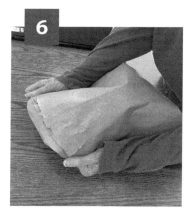

At this point, it is better to push the bag in on all sides to form the ball; it may take several pushes to form the shape into a round ball rather than a football.

Cover the ball with duct tape, and be sure the ball is completely covered.

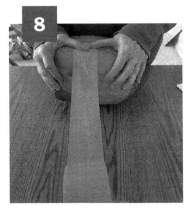

This is better accomplished by working in twos, one person holding and stretching the tape and one person cutting the tape.

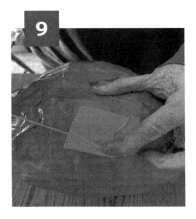

When the ball is finished, take a long piece of heavy string and attach it to the ball with more duct tape.

The bag is now complete and ready to be hung somewhere to be used as a way to release your anger by hitting it over and over again.

Hit the mad bag.

Hitting the Mad Bag with force

Finished Product

Rather than hitting someone else, this tool can help keep someone from striking out at another person or object. This is not a toy, but rather a therapeutic tool. This is also a wonderful activity for families to come together, make this bag or bags, and to laugh, cry, and release their energy and stress of the day.

APPENDIX B

"The Dash"

As we remember those who have gone before us, it is also important for us to realize that someday we, too, will be remembered. Our legacy awaits us. As we remember the birth and death dates of our loved ones, we should also focus on the lives they lived. Linda Ellis wrote the poem "The Dash," which reminds us to consider not just the birth and death dates, but also to consider the dash—the time between our birth and death dates that represents our lives: who we are and what we did. The dash is the time that really matters.

THE DASH
By Linda Ellis

I read of a man who stood to speak at the funeral of
a friend. He referred to the dates on the tombstone
from the beginning ... to the end.
He noted that first came the date of birth and spoke of
the following date with tears, but he said what mattered
most of all was the dash between those years.

For that dash represents all the time they spent alive on earth and
now only those who loved them know what that little line is worth.
For it matters not, how much we own, the
cars ... the house ... the cash. What matters is how
we live and love and how we spend our dash.
So think about this long and hard; are there things
you'd like to change? For you never know how
much time is left that still can be rearranged.
To be less quick to anger and show appreciation more and
love the people in our lives like we've never loved before.
If we treat each other with respect and more often wear a smile ...
remembering that this special dash might only last a little while.
So when your eulogy is being read, with your life's
actions to rehash, would you be proud of the things
they say about how you lived your dash?

© 1996–2020 Southwestern Inspire Kindness, Inc. All Rights Reserved.
By Linda Ellis, Copyright © 2020 Inspire
Kindness, thedashpoem.com

APPENDIX C

Grief and the Holidays

One of the problems for the bereaved during the holidays is that the holiday season seems to go on and on. The department stores start advertising several months before the actual holiday. For example: have you ever walked into a store in August and seen Halloween costumes or in October and seen Thanksgiving and Christmas items or at the end of December and seen Valentine hearts everywhere you look? I have and it is very stressful.

Everyone is looking forward to the holidays, so why aren't we? The answer is simple: a part of us is dead. A part of us is missing. A part of us is empty. When our loved one died or was killed, a part of us died with them. A part that can never be replaced by another child, another spouse, another parent or another sibling. WE can never go back to the way we were, because we are not the same person that we used to be.

There is an old saying: When a child dies, a part of our future dies, because of all the plans we had for that child or because of all the potential we saw in that child. When a spouse dies, a part of our past, present and future dies. When a parent dies, a part of our past dies and when both parents die, it's like feeling you are orphaned.

So, what makes society and advertisers think everyone is ready, willing, and able for the holidays to begin? Because we live in a death dying society, no one wants to talk with or deal with someone who is crying, confused, upset or sad because of a death. Unless you are bereaved or have been bereaved, you may not have a clue as to what someone who is bereaved may be feeling.

Someone in my grief group at the hospital told me: "We are a group of people who belong to a very exclusive club that no one wanted to join, but each one has paid the dearest price on earth to join." How sad, but how true.

When we grieve, we grieve not only the person who has died, but also the life that we have lived and loved with that person. We grieve the happy times, the sad times, the important times and the not so important times that we were together. We also grieve those very special times during the holidays that we were together; those Kodak moments, special rituals, customs and traditions that we shared year after year. All of this is interwoven into the many memories of our loved ones. Just the thought of a first holiday or another holiday without our loved one can be almost unbearable for the bereaved.

Just hearing the sounds of the approaching holidays can bring us to our knees. We are constantly being reminded that our lives have changed and will never be the same again. We may feel disconnected with our family and our friends, but yet we try to be happy when we are really feeling, so empty and alone inside. Sometimes even being in a crowd can be lonely.

We may feel like the nursery rhyme Humpty Dumpty, who was in so many pieces they didn't know what to do or how to put him back together again. Perhaps what we need to do, is rearrange those pieces and try to put them back together in a different form. Since, we can't go back, we need to live with what we've got and move forward step by step, day by day, hour by hour. On those rough days, when it is hard to even put one foot in front of the other, we need to find someone to talk to or just spend some time alone and just relax and wait for a better and softer moment to move forward.

Sometimes we run away from our grief by trying to keep busy and very active, so that we don't have to deal with the pain of our loss. The problem with that is, when we do slow down, our grief is there waiting for us to return. So, what can we do to get through the holidays, birthdays, anniversaries and other special occasions?

Here are some suggestions to help you get through the holidays:

- BE PATIENT WITH YOURSELF AND THOSE AROUND YOU. DON'T PUT EXPECTATIONS ON YOURSELF OR OTHERS.
- HAVE A PLAN OR TWO as to what you might be doing over the holidays and then tell your plan to your friends and family so they know what they might expect from you. If you are invited to do something you'd rather not do, be tentative but honest in giving your answer. An honest explanation of how you have been feeling lately might help explain your answer of hesitating.
- IT IS OK TO CHANGE YOUR TRADITION. Perhaps, having Thanksgiving or Christmas dinner at a different house or going out for dinner instead of cooking might be a good change for this year. The more you try to make it the same as it was before, the more obvious your loved one's absence will be.
- COUNTER THE CONSPIRACY OF SILENCE by talking about your loved one. Because your family and friends love you, they may think they are doing you a favor by not mentioning your loved one for fear you will be upset. You can break the silence by mentioning him/her yourself and explain to them how important it is to you to be able to remember your loved one during the holidays. This could invite others to join in and tell a story or memory of your loved one as well.
- FIND A CREATIVE OUTLET TO REMEMBER YOUR LOVED ONE. You could write a memorial poem or story about your loved one and share it with others. Contribute to or work with a group that your loved one supported. Use the money that you would have spent for a gift for that special person, to buy something for someone he or she cared about.

- CONSIDER CUTTING BACK ON YOUR CARD SENDING. It is not really necessary to send cards to people you will see over the holidays.
- HOLIDAYS often magnify feelings of the loss of a loved one. It is important and natural to experience the sadness that comes during the holidays. To try to block those feelings is unhealthy. Please keep the positive memory of your loved one alive and just feel what you feel and don't try to hide it. If you are going to someone's house for dinner, you might explain to them before you get there, that this might be a difficult day for you and you might need to step out for a few minutes. This way they are aware of what could happen and they don't panic if it does happen.
- TRY attending holiday services at a different time or even a different church.
- EMOTIONALLY, PHYSICALLY AND PSYCHOLOGICALLY, THE HOLIDAYS ARE DRAINING. You need every bit of strength and rest you can get.
- SOME PEOPLE FEAR crying in public, especially at a church service. However, it is really ok to cry. You should try to be gentle with yourself. If you do cry, you will probably feel better. If you need to get up and leave for a short time, it is ok—perhaps you might even feel better to sit in a different place when you return.
- SET LIMITATIONS. Realize, that the holidays are NOT going to be easy. Do the things that are very special and important to you. If you don't feel like shopping this year and being attacked by Santa's elves, then try shopping through the internet or a catalog or just give gift certificates. You could even give a donation to the charity of your choice in memory of your loved one.
- YOU might buy a small tree and an ornament for that tree that reminds you of your loved one. Every year add another ornament to this special tree. Or you could have a special stocking and fill it with things that remind you of your loved one.

- Often after the first year, the people in your life may expect you to be "over it", however, you never "Get Over It," rather you get through your grief. Everyone may expect you to be happy and excited like they are about the holidays and can't seem to understand what is taking you so long. What they don't understand is that, there is no time limit when you have lost a piece of your heart. So, hold on to Hope and please don't give up. You will get through the holidays.
- It may seem after reading all of this, that the holidays will be horrendous. Yes, you may have some difficult times, but you certainly can experience some joy as well. Having a good time and laughing does not mean you have forgotten your loved one or that you loved him/her any less. Just remember, Anticipation of any holiday, birthday, or anniversary is much worse than the actual day. So, take a breath, relax and try to enjoy what you can and the rest will take care of itself. Blessing to all of you!!!!!!!!!!!!!!!!!!!!!!!!!

APPENDIX D

Why Don't We Say Their Name

Several people have written poems on "Saying the name of a person or telling a story about a loved one after they have died." These poems are vital to most of the bereaved, because they explain what it means to someone bereaved to hear their loved one's name mentioned and to know that they are not forgotten.

It seems however, there is a myth, that if someone should mention the name or a memory of the bereaved deceased loved one's they will be hurt, sad or even be devastated to hear this. However, the truth is just the opposite.

Why don't we say their names or talk about them after a death? Is it that we are afraid it will hurt or upset their loved ones who are left? Is it that we are too busy with our own lives, that we have moved on? Is it that we just don't care? Is it that we just don't feel comfortable talking about someone who has died? WoW!! Whatever the reason------it is just plain wrong.

After our loved one dies it is so important to know that they will not be forgotten by others. When we hear others talk about them, hear their name mentioned or hear stories about them it feels good and gives us hope to know they will not be forgotten and perhaps that they even made a difference in this crazy world we live in.

I believe we live in a death denying society where people are afraid to talk about someone who died or even afraid to reach out to friends or family of those who have died. All of this is so sad because the bereaved are the ones who are truly suffering from the loss of their loved one and many times the support they need and want is just not given. A simple word, a kind gesture would certainly go a long way to reassure the bereaved they are not alone in their grief.

As a grief therapist and chaplain working at a hospital with two grief groups and one SOS (Survivors of Suicide- a grief group for family and friends of those whose loved one has already completed a suicide), I have heard and seen the pain and anger in the voices and on the faces of the bereaved over many years especially concerning this issue. They are lost, lonely and longing to hear someone talk about their loved one in a conversation, or hear a story or memory about them that perhaps they had not heard before or even a familiar memory of their loved one.

The pain they feel is very real and very deep. Their sadness, anxiety and anger they experience is at times overwhelming. The bereaved simply cannot understand why their friends, family or even colleagues and physicians don't mention their deceased loved ones when they talk with them.

The bereaved are hurt and angry because most people Do Not realize or take the time to realize just how important this issue is to the bereaved. A couple of years ago, someone in one of my groups whose wife had died, had pictures and cards made of his wife for a family Thanksgiving gathering. Those who were present were their adult daughter, their grandson, son-in-law, aunt, his wife's sister and several cousins. He was very excited to share the pictures with his family. However, no one said a word about the pictures or about his wife, even though all were related and loved her dearly. No stories, no memories, no mention of her name — it was like she didn't even exist. He was hurt, extremely angry and very upset with those gathered there. Yes, they were grieving but even if they had shed a tear, mentioned her name or remembered her in a memory he would have been happy----but nothing. So, you see even some families have a problem with what to say, even when it is their own family.

A couple of weeks ago, I asked a couple of medical professionals and a financial advisor what their thoughts were concerning this bereavement issue. The first one said: it made him feel uncomfortable to talk about someone who died, so he didn't say anything. How sad! I suggested he rethink his thoughts. I then explained to him how it important it was to the bereaved to hear their loved one's name, he said he had no idea, and he would try to rethink his own personal uncomfortableness and not let that get in the way next time he is in that situation.

The second medical professional said she understood exactly what I was talking about. When her dad died, it made her and her mother and family feel so good that so many talked about her dad and told stories about him that they had never heard before. She said, it made her young son, very happy that so many people remembered his grandpa.

The financial advisor said, when he went to the funeral of a friend, he wore a certain Hawaiian shirt that his friend would have worn at one time, in memory of his friend. His friend's wife recognized the shirt at once as being something her husband would have worn and she smiled.

If only more families, friends, and professionals would take the time to share a memory with the bereaved about their deceased loved one, perhaps, they too would come to understand what it means to the bereaved to know that their loved one's will not be forgotten but rather live on in their memories as well as others.

So, what can we do to reach out to the bereaved? First, it is extremely important for the bereaved to talk about their loved ones around other people which in turn will give others permission to talk about them with the bereaved.

Next, everyone else, simply needs to talk about the bereaved loved one in a conversation or relate a story or share a memory of what you remember about them. By doing this you are bringing them joy that their loved one has not been forgotten and that others really do care about them. If the bereaved do break down and cry, they are tears of happiness that their loved one is being remembered. Also please be patient with them and think, how that would make you feel if your loved one died and no one remembered your loved one?

It is sad to think that sometimes, someone in a family or a friend has to die before someone else actually understands what the bereaved go through. As my grief groups would say, THEY JUST DON'T GET IT!!!!

GLOSSARY

Acquire Immune Deficiency (AIDS). This condition consists of certain leukocytes, resulting in infection, cancer, neural degeneration, and possibly HIV.

altruistic suicide. Giving one's life for others or for a greater good; also referred to as "self-destruction demanded by a society."

Alzheimer's disease. A degenerative brain disease.

Amyotrophic Lateral Sclerosis (ALS). A disease of the nerve cells in the brain and spinal cord that control voluntary muscle movement; also known as Lou Gehrig's disease.

anomic suicide. The relationship between an individual and a society, when society is suddenly shattered or disrupted.

autism. A developmental disorder marked by impaired social interactions and communication difficulties.

bereaved. Individuals who are left behind after a death.

bereavement. "To be torn apart." It also refers to the period of mourning after a loss, especially after the death of a loved one.

cerebral palsy. A muscular disorder resulting from damage to the nervous system especially at birth.

complicated grief reactions. Or complicated mourning. Abnormal grief or mourning processes leading to deviant and unhealthy maladaptive behaviors and inhibiting progress toward satisfactory outcomes in mourning.

dash. Metaphor for a person's life between their birth date and death date.

Down syndrome. A congenital condition characterized by mental deficiency.

egotistic suicide. An individual's mental energies concentrated on the self to such an extent that social sanctions against suicide are ineffective.

empty nest syndrome. When the child or children leave to go to college or get married and the house is empty except for the parent or parents left behind. It can be devastating for the individuals left behind.

euphemisms. A word or phrase that is considered less offensive, such as "remains" for *a corpse* or "kicked the bucket" for *died*.

fatalistic suicide. Excessive social constraints, lack of freedom, and absence of choice causing someone to want to escape from such a society.

genogram. Tracing a person's family history—like a family tree.

grief. The normal emotional reactions to a loss.

mad bag. A punching bag used to help the bereaved release their anger.

mourning. Going public with someone's grief or loss.

perinatal. The loss pertaining to the periods before, during, or after the times of birth. For example: miscarriage, stillborn, or induced abortion.

Post Traumatic Stress Disorder (PTSD). A stress response resulting from experiencing traumatic events.

psychache. The unbearable mental pain that is caused by the frustration of a person's most important needs that are unique to each individual. This could possibly lead to suicide.

Shiva. The seven days of mourning after a Jewish funeral.

Sudden Infant Death Syndrome (SIDS). A death of an apparently healthy infant, usually before one year of age, and of unknown or undetermined cause.

triggers. Events that occur after a death that can upset the bereaved, such as birthdays, anniversaries, or someone who resembles the deceased.

yarmulke. A skullcap worn especially by Orthodox and conservative Jewish males in the synagogue and the home.

BIBLIOGRAPHY

Adamec, C. (2000). *When your pet dies: Dealing with your grief and helping your children cope.* Lincoln, NE: iUniverse.

Adamson, D. (2010). *Requirement for death, dying and bereavement course: The mad bag.* Northcentral University: Arizona.

Allen, M.A. (2014). Ten Tips on Coping with Pet Loss. http://www.pet-loss.net.

Allen, M. A. (2014). The Emotions of Pet Loss. http://pet-loss.net/emotions.shtml.

Anderson, R. (1974). Notes of a survivor. In S. B. Green (Ed.), *The patient, death and the family* New York: Oxford University Press.

Barrett, R. K. (1997). Bereaved Black children. In J. Morgan (Ed.), *Readings in thanatology.* Amityville, NY: Baywood.

Benham, K. (2005). The good listener. *St. Petersburg Times*, p. E1.

Blow, F.C. *Substance abuse among older adults: Treatment improvement protocol.* (Tip) series #26, Rockville, MD: U.S. Dept. of Health and Human Services.

Breck, J. (1995). Euthanasia and the quality of life debate. *Christian Bioethics 1,* 322–337.

Brogden, M. (2001). *Genocide.* London and Philadelphia: Jessica Kingsley Publishers.

Cable, D. (2000). Grief in the American culture. In K. J. Doka & J. D. Davidson (Eds.), *Living with grief: Who we are How we grieve* (pp. 61–70). Philadelphia, P: Hospice Foundation of America.

Campbell, S., & Silverman, P. R. (1996). *Widower: When men are left alone.* Amityville, NY: Baywood.

Conwell, Y. (2001). Suicide in later life: A review and recommendations for prevention. *Suicide and Life-threatening Behavior,* 31–46.

Cook, A. S., & Dworkin, D. S. (1992). *Helping the bereaved: Therapeutic interventions for children, adolescents and adults.* New York: Basic Books.

Cook, J. A., & Wimberly, D. W. (1983). If I should die before I wake: Religious commitment and adjustment to the death of a child. *Journal for Scientific Study of Religion 22,* 222–238.

Corr, C. A. (1998). Enhancing the concept of disenfranchised grief. *Omega, 38,* 1–20.

Corr, C. A., Nabe, C. M., & Corr, D. M. (2000). *Death and dying, life and living* (3rd ed.). Belmont, CA: Wadsworth.

Davies, B. (1985). Behavioral responses of children to the death of a sibling. *Final report submitted to Alberta Foundation for Nursing Research.* Edmonton, Alberta.

DeSpelder, L. A., & Strickland, A. L. (2014). *The last dance: Encountering death and dying*. Mountain View; CA: Mayfield.

Doka, K. J. (2002). *Living with grief: Loss in later life*. Washington, D.C: Hospice Foundation of America.

Durkheim, E. (1951). *Suicide: A study in sociology*. New York: Free Press.

Dyregrov, K. & Dyregrov, A. (2005). Helping the family following suicide. In B. Monroe & F. Kraus (Eds.), *Brief interventions with bereaved children* Oxford: Oxford University Press.

Ellis, L. (1996). *The Dash*. Southwestern Inspire Kindness, Inc. thedashpoem.com

Everly Jr., G. S., Latin, J. M., & Mitchell, J. T. (2000). Innovations in group crisis intervention. In A. R. Roberts (Ed.), *Crisis intervention handbook: Assessment, treatment and research* (2nd ed.), New York: Oxford University Press.

Feldman, D. M., & Rosner, F. (1984). *Compendium on medical ethics* (6th ed.). New York: Federation of Jewish Philanthropies of New York.

Foy, D. W., Glynn, S. M., Schnurr, P. P., Jankowski, M. K., Wattenberg, M. S., Weiss, D. S., Marmar, C. R., & Gusman, F. D. (2000). In E. B. Foa, T. M. & M.J. Freidman (Eds.), *Effective treatments for PTSD* . New York: Guilford Press.

Fulton, R., & Owen, G. (1987). Death & society in the twentieth century America. *Omega: Journal of Death & Dying*, 18(4).

Funerals and religious customs (2006). http://www.a-to-z-of-manners-and-etiquette.com.

Furman, R. A. (1973). A child's capacity for mourning. In E. J. Anthony & C. Koupernik (Eds.), *The child in his family: The impact of disease and death* (pp. 225–231). New York: Wiley.

Gallagher-Thompson, D. & Colleagues (1993). The impact of spousal bereavement on older widows and widowers. In M.S. Strobe, W. Stroebe, & R.O. Hansson, (Eds.), *Handbook of bereavement: Theory, research and interventions* (pp. 227–239). New York: Cambridge University Press.

Gamino, L., & Ritter, H. (2009). Ethical practice in grief counseling. New York: Spring.

Goldenberg, J. & Colleagues (1999). Death, sex, love and neuroticism: Why is sex such a problem? *Journal of Personality & Social Psychology, 77*(6), 1173–1187.

Gross, R., & Klass, D. (1997). Tibetan Buddhism and the resolution of grief: the bardo-thodol for the dying and the grieving. *Death Studies, 21,* 377–395.

Hageman, W. (2013). Pets grieve too. *Chicago Tribune,* July 16, pp. 1–3.

Hanh, T. N. (2001). Waking up the nation. *Tricycle: The Buddhist Review, XI*(2), 23.

Harvey, A. D. (1986). Evidence of a tense shift in personal experiences narratives. *Empirical Studies of the Arts 4*(2), 151–162.

Heddtke, L., & Winslade, J. (2004). The use of the subjunctive in remembering conversations with those who are grieving. *Omega: Journal of Death & Dying, 50*(3), 197–215.

Insel, P., & Roth, W. (2013). *Connect core concepts in health* (13th ed.). New York: McGraw-Hill.

Johnson, C. J., & McGee, M. G. (Eds.). (1991). *How different religions view death and afterlife.* Philadelphia: Charles Press.

Kalish, R. A., & Reynolds, D. K. (1976). *Death and Ethnicity: A psychocultural study.* Los Angeles: Ethel Percy Andrus Gerontology Center.

Kamel, H. K., Mouton, C. P., & McKee, D. R. (2001). Culture and loss. In *Living with Grief: Loss in later life* (pp. 282–294). Washington, D. C.: Hospice Foundation of America.

Kanner, L. (1943). Autistic disturbances of affective contact. *Nervous Child, 2,* 217–250.

Kastenbaum, R., & Aisenberg, R. (1976). *The psychology of death.* New York: Springer.

Kellehear, A. (2005). *Compassionate cities: Public health and end-of-life care.* New York: Routledge.

Keown, D. (1995). *Buddhism and bioethics.* New York: St. Martin's Press.

King, B. (2013). *How animals grieve.* Chicago: University of Chicago Press.

Kloeppel, D. A., & Hollis, S. (1989). Double handicap: Mental retardation and death in the family. *Death Studies, 13,* 31–38.

Lagoni, L., Butler, C., & Hett, S. (1994). *The human-animal bond and grief.* Philadelphia, PA: W.B. Saunders.

Luchterhand, C., & Murphy, N. (1998). *Helping adults with mental retardation grieve a death loss.* Bristol, PA: Accelerated Development.

Lund, D. A. (1989). *Older bereaved spouses: Research with practical applications*. New York: Taylor & Francis.

Lund, D. A., Diamond, M. S., & Shafer, S. K. (1989). Competencies, tasks of daily living and adjustments to spousal bereavement in later life. In D. A. Lund (Ed.), *Older bereaved spouses: Research with practical applications*. New York: Taylor & Francis/Hemisphere.

Marshall, V. (1980). *Last Chapter: A sociology of aging and dying*. Monterey, CA: Brooks/Cole.

Maurice, J. (2013). Mitigating disasters – A promising start. *The Lancer, 381*(9878), 1611–1613.

McGee, M. (1981). Faith, fantasy and flowers: A content analysis of the American sympathy card. *Omega: Journal of Death & Dying, 11*(1), 27–29.

Meagher, D. (2002). Ethical & legal issues in traumatic death. In *Handbook of Thanatology*. (2nd ed.) (pp. 311–320). New York: Harper & Row.

Miller, M. (1985). Suicide prevention. Franciscan Medical Center, *Address to Health Care Professionals & Clergy*. Rock Island, Illinois.

Moss, M., & Moss. S. (1983). The impact of parental death on middle aged children. *Omega: Journal of Death & Dying 14*, 65–67.

Motto, J. (1999). Critical points in the assessment and management of suicide risk. In D. G. Jacobs (Ed.), *The Harvard Medical School guide to suicide assessment and intervention* (pp. 224–238). San Francisco: Jossey-Bass

Noel, B., & Blair, P. D. (2000). *I wasn't ready to say goodbye*. Vancouver, WA: Champion Press.

Nouwen, H. (2014). *Wait for the Lord*. Fenton, MO: Creative Communications for the Parish.

Ochs, D. J. (1993). *Consolatory rhetoric: Grief symbols and rituals in the Greco-Roman era*. Columbus: University of South Carolina Press.

Osgood, N. (1992). *Suicide in later life*. New York: Lexington Books.

Palmer, B. (2009). Will your dog mourn your death? *The Washington Post*, pp. 1–7.

Pan American Health Organization: *Management of dead bodies in situations*. Washington, D.C: PAHO.

Parkes, C. M. (2001). *Bereavement: Studies of grief in adult life*. (3rd ed.). New York: Routledge.

Pearson, J. (2000). Suicidal behavior in later life. In R. Maris, S.J. Canetto, J. McIntosh, & J. Silverman (Eds.), *Review of Suicidology 2000* (pp. 202–225). New York: Guilford.

Phillips, S. (2013). *Do we recognize the grief of losing a sibling?* University of Phoenix: WGBH Educational Foundation & Vulcan Productions Inc.

Piaget, J. (1954). *The construction of reality in the child*. New York: Basic Books.

Plumley, R. P. (2007). *When a teen is grieving*. One Caring Place. Indiana: Abbey Press.

Rahman, F. (1987). *Health and medicine in the Islamic tradition: Change and identity*. New York: Crossroad.

Rando, T. A. (1993). The treatment of complicated mourning. Champaign, IL: Research Press.

Rando, T. A. (1996). In K. J. Doka (Ed.), *Living with grief after sudden loss: Suicide, homicide, accident, heart attack, and stroke.* Washington, D.C.: Riyish.

Robinson, L., Segal, J., & Segal, R. (2013). Coping with Pet Loss. *Help guide for ages 1–6.* https://wwwhelpguide.org/articles/grief/copingwith losing a pet.htm?pdf=13251.

Rynearson, E. K. (1978). Humans and pets and attachments. *The Journal of British Psychiatry, 133*, 550–555.

School of manners & common sense (2006). https://www.a-to-zof manners-and-etiquette.com.

Shneidman, E. S. (1993). Suicide as psychache. *Journal of Nervous and Mental Diseases, 181*(3), 147–149.

Silverman, P. R., & Klass, D. (1996). *Introduction: What's the problem? Continuing bonds: New understandings in grief.* Washington, DC: Taylor & Francis.

Stein, E., & Eisen, B. (1996). Helping trauma survivors cope: Effects of immediate brief co-therapy and crisis intervention. *Crisis Intervention, 3*, 113–127.

Stengel, E. (1969) A matter of communication. In E. S. Sheidman (Ed.), *On the nature of suicide* San Francisco: Jossey-Boss.

Stephenson, J. (1985). *Death, grief and mourning: Individual and social realities.* New York: Free Press.

Stewart, M. F. (1999). *Companion animal deaths: A practical and comprehensive guide for veterinary practice.* Woburn, MA: Butterworth-Hernemann Medical.

Talamanto, M. A., Gomez, C., & Braun, K. L. (2000). Advances directives and end-of-life care: The Hispanic perspective. In K. L. Braun, J.H. Pietsch, & P.L. Blanchette (Eds.), *Cultural Issues in end-of-life decision making.*. Thousand Oaks, CA: Sage Publications.

Tamir, L. (1982). *Men in their forties: The transition to middle age.* New York: Springer.

White, P. G. (2006). *Sibling grief: Healing after the death of a sister or brother.* Lincoln, NE: iUniverse.

Widdison, H., & Salisbury, H. (1989). The delayed stress syndrome: A pathological delayed grief reaction. *Omega: Journal of Death & Dying, 20*(4), 293–306.

Williams, M. B., & Nurmi, L. A. (1997). Death of a co-worker: Facilitating the healing. In C. R. Figley, B. E. Bride & N. Mazza (Eds.), *Death and Trauma: The traumatology of grieving.* Bristol, PA: Taylor & Francis.

Wolfelt, A. D. (2006). When your pet dies. *Butler Funeral Homes (Pet Services).* Springfield, Illinois.

Worden, J. W. (1982). *Grief counseling and grief therapy: A handbook for the mental health practitioner.* New York: Springer.

Worden, J. W. (1996). *Children and grief: When a parent dies.* New York: Gilford.

ANNOTATED REFERENCES

Allen, N. H. & Peek, M. L. (1975). *Suicide and young people.* A brochure prepared by the American Association of Suicidology.

This small brochure explains the four things that suicidal teens need to be aware of and how to help them get through this difficult time.

Anderson, R. (1968). *I never sang for my father.* New York: Dramatists Play Service.

This play suggests that "death ends a life, but it does not end a relationship." This is another way to say that continuing a relationship with the deceased is very important and can heal the bereaved in many ways. Having that continuous bond with someone who died will help keep them and their memory alive for the bereaved and their family.

Boss, P. (1999). *Ambiguous loss.* Cambridge MA: Harvard University Press.

Boss takes disenfranchised grief a step further and introduces ambiguous loss and the uncertainty that this type of loss entails. Ambiguous loss centers around two main types: physically absent but psychologically present and physically present but psychologically absent.

Bowlby, J. (1980). *Attachment and loss: Loss, sadness and depression.* New York: Basic Books.

In this book Bowlby discusses how to help those mentally challenged individuals that are bereaved. He suggests five important actions that can be achieved to help these bereaved individuals to cope: (1) Tell the person the death has transpired; (2) Encourage and allow the person to share their feeling;(3) Reassure the bereaved individual they are not alone, that others are there to help them; (4) Be patient with the person grieving; they should not be rushed in their grief; (5) It is important to listen to the bereaved and learn from them so they can be helped now and in the future.

Brett, M., & Davis, E. M. B. (1998.) What does it mean? Sibling and parental appraisals of childhood leukemia. *Cancer Nursing 11,* 329–338.

Brett and Davis suggest three variables which could contribute to sibling responses and help them to understand and to deal with the loss of their sibling. These are (1) the type of death; (2) closeness of the two siblings; (3) family social climate. He also states that society does not sanction or support the loss of a sibling, which could make their time of grieving and mourning even difficult for a sibling whose brother/sister died.

Bryson, B. (2001). *The mother tongue: English and how it got that way. 189.* New York: Perennial.

Bryson does a wonderful job discussing the language people use when they are speaking about death and dying. The examples he gives in this article are right on target.

Clayton, P. J. (1974). Mortality and morbidity in the first year of widowhood. *Archives of General Psychiatry, 30*, 747–750.

Clayton discusses how the second year of grief can be and often is worse than the first year, because it brings home the finality of the first years' experience to the bereaved. This can be very distressing and difficult for the bereaved especially when they think "If only I can get through the first year, I'll be OK."

Corr, C. (1992). A task-based approach to coping with dying. *Omega, Journal of Death and Dying, 24*, 81–94.

Dr. Corr discusses the four areas of tasks that take place after a public tragedy: Physical, psychological, social and spiritual and how these four areas affect the bereaved.

Davies, B. (1999). *Shadows in the sun: Experiences of sibling bereavement in childhood*. Philadelphia, PA.: Brunner-Mozel.

Davies discusses how the impact of sibling bereavement can last a lifetime, especially when they are feeling as though these four major sibling responses describe them and their situations: (1) "I hurt inside;" (2) "I don't understand;" (3) "I don't belong;" and (4) "I'm not enough."

Dodd, P., Guerin, S., McEvoy, J., Buckley, S. Tyrrell, J., & Hillery, J. (2008). A study of complicated grief symptoms in people with intellectual disabilities. *Journal of Intellectual Disability Research, 52*, 5, 415–425.

Dodd and his colleagues suggest that those with intellectual disabilities can be taught words as well as actions that show sympathy. They also discuss the importance of rituals for these individuals and how these rituals can help them to cope with a death.

Doka, K. J. (1989). *Disenfranchised grief: Recognizing hidden sorrows.* Lexington, MA: Lexington Books.

Dr. Doka suggest that those who are disenfranchised go past the boundaries of what society considers acceptable deaths such as suicide, divorce, death of a pet, triangle love affair, perinatal deaths.

Farberow, N. L. (1991). Adult survivors after suicide: Research problems and needs In A. Leenaars (Ed.), *Life span perspectives of suicide process.* New York: Plenum.

Farberow deals with the older generation and how they are often forgotten by family and friends. This emptiness could lead to completing a suicide without their family ever realizing what happened. The research also recommends two emotions (identification with the suicide and loss of trust) that survivors need to deal with in order to understand what happened to their loved one.

Folta, C., & Deck, D. (1976). Grief, the funeral and the friend. In V. Pine, A.H. Kutsscher, and Peretz, R.C. (Eds.), *Acute grief and the funeral.* Springfield, IL: Charles C. Thomas.

Folta and Deck discuss the four main categories that fall under disenfranchised grief. When a death does occur from these types of death they are not supported by society or employers. They are usually left on their own to deal with their grief.

Hofsees, R. (2002). Grief and loss in the workplace. *The Forum: Association of Death Education and Counseling.*

According to Hofsess, employees need six things from their employers to help them grieve the loss of a loved one. He also discusses some estimated costs of ignoring and not supporting grief in the workplace.

Klass, D., Silverman, P. R., & Nickman, S. L. (1996). *Continuing bonds: New understandings of grief.* Washington, D.C: Taylor & Francis.

Dennis Klass and his colleagues state that is very important for the bereaved to keep an ongoing connection to their loved one even after they have died. They also stated that this type of connection develops solace, comfort, support, and eases the transition from the past to the future. By talking about and remembering our loved ones, we will be able to get through our very difficult times.

Kodanz, R. (2000). *Grief in the workplace bereavement.* Colorado Springs, CO: Bereavement Publishing.

Kodanz explains the complexity in the workplace when a co-worker dies. He also discusses the challenges and difficulties fellow employees experience and how they can be helped.

Kosins, M. S. (1996). *Maya's first rose: diary of a very special love.* New York: Routledge.

Martin Kosins explains: If you have ever loved an animal, then there are three days in your life you will always remember.

Kubler-Ross, E., & Kessler, D. (2005). *On grief and grieving.* New York: Scribner.

This entire book is an excellent resource on grief and grieving and death and dying. Each chapter was clear and concise and very rich in material on the subject. The chapter on children explains that children need to be told the truth when a loved one is dying and should be allowed to spend time with that person. It is very important for them to be able to say their goodbyes to their loved one just as adults do.

Nelson, R. E., & Galas, J. C. (1994). *The power to prevent suicide.* Minneapolis MN: Free Spirit Publishing Co.

This is a wonderful reference for teens and suicide. It discusses two main types of threats made by teens as well as seven warning signs to be aware of and how to reach out to these teens.

Plopper, B. L., & Ness, M. E. (1993). Death as portrayed to adolescents through Top 40 rock and roll music, *Journal on Adolescence 28,* 793–807.

Often teens see death as it is portrayed in the entertainment media, such as video games, movies, and the changing music scene. There have several crimes where someone followed the advice on a video game or movie and tried to kill or hurt someone because they thought the video game or movie told them to do so.

Rando, T. (1993). *The treatment of complicated mourning.* Champaign, IL: Research Press.

Dr. Rando has suggested nine warning signs and complicating factors in grief to be aware of concerning mentally challenged bereaved individuals and how to help these individuals.

Rathkey, J.W. (2004). *What children need when they grieve.* New York: Three Rivers Press.

In this well written book, Rathkey explains a healthy approach as to how bereaved adolescents often cope with the loss of a loved one by listening to music, writing a song or memory of the person who died, poetry or prose or artwork.

Robinson, L., Segal J., & Segal, R. (2013). Coping with Pet Loss: Grieving the death of a dog or cat and moving on. http://www.helpguide.org/mental/grieving-pets.htm.

These authors remind us that everyone grieves differently and that the grief of the loss of our pet is very personal to us. Not everyone loves our pet as we do, but if we deal with this negativity and remember our love for this pet, we will be able to get through this very difficult loss. Reaching out to others who have explained a loss of their pet is very important as well.

Strickland, A. (2014). *Familicide in the A-Z of death and dying*: Social medical and cultural aspects. (Ed.). Santa Barbara, CA: ABC-CL10/Greenwood.

Strickland discusses the fact that so many family members are killing family members due to many stressful situations. This form of killing family members is known as familicide. It also covers the killings of brothers, sisters, spouses, mothers, fathers and children.

Tate, F. B. (1989). Impoverishment of death symbolism: The negative consequences. *Death Studies, 13*(3), 305–306.

Tate does an excellent job discussing how television programming and movies can influence our lives concerning death and dying. He explains how listening and watching television or some movies can give us a different perspective on death that is not true to life. The negative aspects of death are often portrayed in the movies as well as video games.

Worden, J. W. (2002). *Grief counseling and grief therapy: A handbook for the mental health practitioner* (3rd ed.). New York: Springer.

This is one of the great books for those in the mental health field. Worden discusses four types of complicated grief that exist for the bereaved and how to help them get the help they need.

Wortman, C. (2009). Getting through the holiday: Advice for the bereaved. *University of Phoenix: WGBH Educational Foundation and Vulcan Productions, Inc.*

> Dr. Camille Wortman warns the bereaved of four holiday season dilemmas to be aware of: Being happy and cheerful; the minefield of social exchange; the complexity of decisions and the ambush. These are dilemmas that the bereaved may run into wherever they go during the holiday season, especially when they are around friends and family.

Zucker, R. (2009). Grieving the death of a co-worker. *Care notes.* St. Meinrad, IN: Abbey Press.

> Zucker explains what management can do to help their employees when another employee dies. If management makes the effort to reach out to their employees, there will be a change in the employees as well as in the workplace.